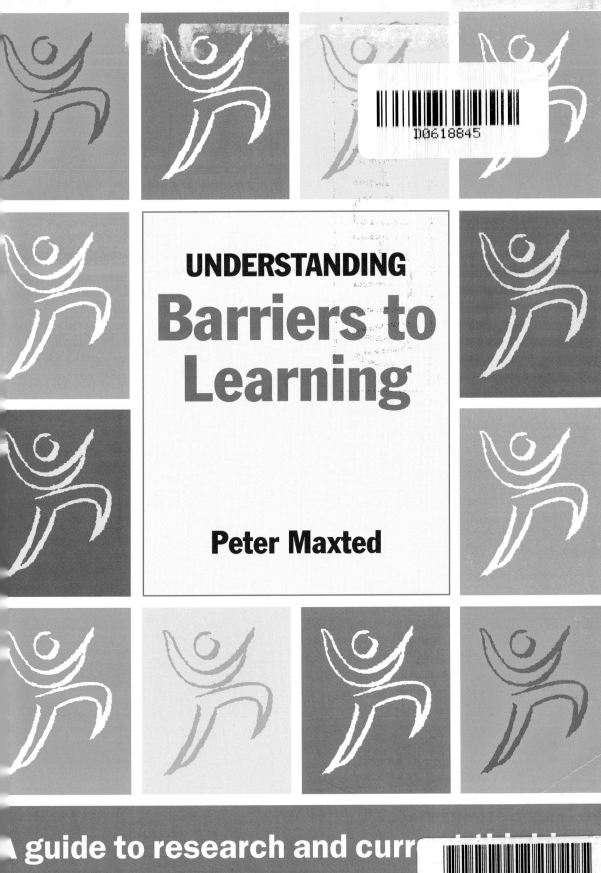

UNDERSTANDING
Barriers to Learning

Peter Maxted

A guide to research and curr...

CAMPAIGN FOR LEARN...

ACKNOWLEDGEMENTS

I WOULD like to thank the Campaign for Learning for giving me the opportunity to produce this guide to the large amount of research that exists on the subject of Barriers to Learning.

I'd also like to thank all those who attended the consultation in 1998 at which this guide was discussed. These were Fiona Morrison, Janet Rice, Chris Quarrie, Brian Stevens, Bridget Widdeson, Gerry Glenister, Anne Simms, Christine Ingall, Alastair Thompson, Mike Caffrey, Dave Eva, Angela Richards, Chris Loveland, Mick Fletcher and Hugh Lloyd-Jones. All the ideas that were put forward at the consultation, concerning both style and content, have been very useful and most have been incorporated.

Particular thanks go to Jim Smith, Andrea Spurling, Alan Tuckett and Ursula Howard who read the penultimate draft of this guide and provided helpful comments.

Finally my thanks to all the team at 't' magazine, especially Rob Ford, for their comments and advice and my partner, Anne Osman, for her unwavering support – especially when I felt I had bitten off considerably more than I could chew!

Peter Maxted

Copyright © Text and Illustrations the Campaign for Learning 1999

First published 1999 by the Campaign for Learning
Campaign for Learning, 19 Buckingham Street, London WC2N 6EF

Produced for the Campaign for Learning by Southgate Publishers Ltd, 15 Barnfield Avenue, Exmouth, Devon EX8 2QE

Printed and bound in Great Britain by Short Run Press Ltd, Devon.

British Library Cataloguing in Publication Data
A CIP catalogue record for this book is available from the British Library.

ISBN 1- 85741- 034-3

CONTENTS

PREFACE

IF WE are to create a Learning Society then nothing short of a revolution is required. While participation rates are rising for some groups of people, if we simply continue on this largely incremental basis we will take far too long. We will have failed too many individuals, especially those who are the least prosperous and the most vulnerable in our society.

There are many good reasons why we as individuals might want to learn. These include fulfilling our need for personal development, increasing our skills, extending our social networks and becoming more employable. But being persuaded that learning is a good thing is not enough. If it were, then far more of us would be active learners; there is a lot more to it than this.

As a campaigning body, we need to understand the barriers that prevent people learning; both for our own purposes and so that we can help facilitate a greater understanding of the issues amongst all those involved. Much excellent research has been carried out and disseminated by trail-blazing organisations like NIACE. But there are also large caverns of unpublished findings which have never seen the light of day, as well as sector and age specific analyses which have never been integrated into an overall picture. Never before, as far as we are aware, has all this research been brought together into one publication.

This book attempts to synthesise and share some of the existing thinking about barriers to learning. It is aimed at anyone interested in promoting learning, from colleges to Citizens Advice Bureaux, policy makers to practitioners. It has been written in a deliberately 'light' style in the hope that it will be of interest to the casual, but interested, reader as well as to experts in specialised areas.

The book has been planned to complement a parallel initiative by one of our partners, the Industrial Society, who will soon be publishing *The Learning Agenda*. That report outlines the findings from qualitative research into people's aspirations for learning at work as well as the barriers which prevent them being fulfilled.

We hope you find this book a useful guide. But most of all, we hope that, having read it, you will go on to take actions to make your sphere a mini learning society.

Barriers to Learning

The new disadvantaged of the twenty-first century will be those who do not have the capacity to learn. It is all of our responsibilities to work to remove the barriers which still prevent learners from learning when, where and how they want to.

Bill Lucas

Bill Lucas
Chief Executive
Campaign for Learning

INTRODUCTION

THE Campaign for Learning is an independent charity with the aim of creating an appetite for learning in every individual and working towards an inclusive society in which learning is valued, understood, wanted and widely available.

Last year the Government published *The Learning Age*[1], setting out a vision of a new society with learning at the very forefront. Every worker a learner, every child a learner, every stakeholder a learner, every citizen a learner – this is the dream.

In order to bring this dream nearer to reality, it is important to understand why some people, in some circumstances, *don't* learn. Is it because they *can't* – due to pressures of time, money or lack of opportunity for example – or because they *won't* – because they think learning is not for them, can't see the benefits or simply couldn't care less?

In his introduction to the 1998 MORI survey[2] on attitudes to learning, Campaign Chief Executive Bill Lucas wrote: "A significant number of us already learn at work, at home or in the community in a variety of different environments. But an equally significant proportion of us are not yet motivated to see learning as important. Or there are factors which make it difficult for us to find the right kind of learning in a location and at a time which suits us."

The survey went on to state: "Despite encouraging developments, the survey corroborates the Campaign's 1996 poll and the findings of the *National Adult Learning Survey*[3] and *The Learning Divide*[4], in showing that certain life factors strongly influence people's attitudes towards, and participation in, learning. Older respondents, people from social class DE[5] households, the retired and those with no qualifications are less likely to currently be involved in learning or to express a desire to be involved in the future. They are also less likely to feel that learning is important or enjoyable."

In 1997, a survey[6] of nearly 5,000 adults confirmed that, "The UK still faces an enormous task in involving all its people in the learning society and that the learning divide between the learning-rich and the learning-poor is growing."

There are an enormous number of barriers to learning. Some of them may be easily overcome – with a little effort on the part of the individual or the company or the state. Some are easily overcome for some people but seem almost insurmountable to others – one man's molehill may be another woman's mountain. And some are virtually hidden – insidious, invisible barriers that the potential learner does not know are there until he or she is sitting dazed in the road with a sore head and bloody nose.

There is an equally enormous amount of work and effort being put in, by many different people and organisations of all shapes and sizes, to overcome the barriers that are in the way of our becoming a learning society.

This book will attempt to identify most of the main barriers to learning by drawing on the existing research into the subject, especially that done in the last ten years. It will arrange these barriers into three main categories and explain why each is important. It is intended that there will soon be a second, complementary guide that will draw on existing good practice to give examples of how barriers to learning can be overcome.

This book will be of use to policy makers and learning practitioners as well as any one, who is, would like to be, or needs to be, a learner.

Organisation

In order to make sense of a vast amount of material, this guide has been broken down into three broad categories of barrier. These are:

Cultural   *Structural*   *Personal*

A number of barriers to learning of course fall into more than one category. For example, under the broad heading 'technology' we find personal barriers (a fear of technology, a 'luddite' mentality, insufficient motor skills to use it, visual disability) structural barriers (lack of quality equipment, inadequate teaching, financial barriers to purchase etc). There are even some *cultural* barriers – many countries and large organisations are uncomfortable with their citizens or workers being empowered to the extent that new technology may allow them to be.

However, all of the barriers identified fall (completely or mainly) into at least one of the three categories. There is a

Introduction ...

similarity of approach with the work of American academic KP Cross who, in 1981 in San Francisco, devised a framework for identifying barriers to adult learning that she described as structural/contextual, institutional, and personal/dispositional.

Policy makers may take the cultural section as the beginning of an exploration into the 'macro' barriers that exist and which need concomitant solutions. Practitioners, teachers, trainers and guidance officers for example, may want to understand better many of the barriers identified in the structural section. Finally, every individual will identify with some of the problems of style and motivation that pervade the third, personal section.

CHAPTER 1

What's in a name?

BEFORE discussing specific barriers to learning (and how they may be overcome) it is necessary to define, briefly, a number of terms. Much terminology is bandied around by people, not least by some policy makers, who may use language lazily and definitions very loosely. So it should be asked, what is the difference between learning, training and education? And who can be defined as a learner and who as a non-learner?

The three degrees
"He is a terrorist,
You are a guerrilla,
I am a freedom fighter."

"He has been trained,
You have been educated,
I am a learner."

Terms such as education, learning, studying and training are often used interchangeably, but they are not one and the same thing.

Education

Most people associate the idea of 'education' with gaining knowledge, a formal foundation for life and work, usually with an element of 'testing' involved. It is seen as being specifically aimed at young people, often associated with school or college and very much a transfer of knowledge from a 'teacher' to a pupil. It is (albeit sometimes wrongly) thought of as passive, involves 'being taught', imposed and prescriptive. Formal education therefore often has negative associations – young learners can feel alienated from a system in which all the 'choices' are made for them.

Within 'formal' education is the idea of 'studying', a concept often viewed as academic and rarefied. It may be linked to specific exams and is quite frequently seen as tedious, difficult and stressful. Studying has been described as the 'hard graft aspect of learning'.

Education, learning, studying and training are often used interchangeably, but they are not one and the same

What's in a name ...?

So what is the difference between learning, training and education?

There is however a clear distinction between formal and informal education. Most people, regardless of their age or social class, see informal education in a positive way. It is closer to the concept of learning.

Training

Training, for the most part, is seen as specific, and tied to a particular skill, task, job or occupation.

While there seems to be a general consensus that training is the development of practical (usually job-related) skills, there is the question of what distinguishes it from simply learning a skill or job by doing it, or by being shown, informally, how to do something. If there is either a 'qualification' (i.e. some kind of formal accreditation) at the end or if it is a requirement for being recognised or employed in a particular field, then the activity is usually considered to be training. Courses, apprenticeships, tests of knowledge or ability and assessment – all play their part.

Again, then, there is a distinction between formal training and informal 'learning'.

Many people associate training with excellence, with 'being the best', and a route into work or to better-paid or higher status jobs. But it is also sometimes considered 'down market', and seen as the poor relation of 'academic' education. It has been defined as 'narrow, over-prescribed or mechanical' and linked to conditioning rather than development. This is particularly true of low level vocational training.

At a different level however we have management training, which is seen as developmental and leading to high-level transferable skills.

The positive or negative perception of training is in the eye of the beholder.

Learning

Learning is much more of an all-embracing concept, and education, studying and training are usually seen as different aspects of learning. It has many positive associations and few negative ones.

Barriers to Learning

Learning is the overall process of acquiring knowledge and skills and a much broader idea than education or training. It is not something that is tied to a particular time of one's life, relevant to only a small social group or otherwise proscriptive.

It has connotations of desire, of being wanted or embraced, 'doing something for the love of it' and has been described as, 'you doing it, not somebody doing it to you'.

Learning is about improving one's quality of life and only incidentally one's quantity of possessions. It is seen as voluntary, broad, open-ended, and covers both the formal and informal acquisition of knowledge. And where education is seen (usually) as being associated with school or college, and generally targeted towards the young, and training is seen as job-specific or skill-related, learning embraces both but goes much wider.

Informal learning takes place at home, at work and in many social situations. The distinction between formal and informal was well summed up last year by David Ashton when he wrote[7]: "In the companies I studied, training was an infrequent activity but learning was an everyday occurrence."

It can include the gaining of social and life skills and, most importantly, includes the desire to *go on* doing it. This is where the idea of lifetime learning comes in – an ongoing process of learning by absorption or osmosis in addition to

What's in a name ...?

being taught or making a conscious effort. As such, lifetime learning involves taking an interest in one's surroundings, reading, talking, watching television, going to the pub, listening to one's children or grandparents, travelling, playing games, building relationships, "Lifetime learning? I'm doing that now."

Learning defined

The definition of learning is being refined all the time. In last years' survey, MORI and the Campaign for Learning made the decision to use the Department for Education and Employment's 1998 *National Adult Learning Survey* definition of learning, which is different to the definition used in the equivalent survey in 1996. The NALS definition (see below) for taught and non-taught learning has been market-tested and was judged to be a reliable definition and effective for research purposes.

- Learning can involve either formal, taught learning or informal, non-taught learning.
- Taught learning, for example, includes training sessions at work, driving lessons, evening classes and teaching yourself using distance learning materials.
- Non-taught learning, for example, includes studying and developing your skills on your own without being enrolled on a course, learning on the job at work, keeping up to date with your own interests by reading books etc.

More associations

Some interesting associations and definitions were brought up by the Campaign's 1998 MORI poll. "As in 1996, 'Gaining knowledge' and 'School' are the words or phrases which first come to mind when people are asked to think about 'Learning' (15% in both cases).

"When asked whether they associate a list of words and phrases with 'Learning', 'Training' or 'Education', 'Discovering' (70%), 'Finding out more' (67%) and 'Enjoyment' (62%) are most frequently associated with 'Learning'.

Barriers to Learning

"As with 'Learning', people spontaneously associate 'Education' with 'School' (24%) and 'Gaining knowledge' (11%). When prompted, people associate 'Education' with 'School' (71%) and 'Studying' (57%). When asked to think about 'Training', adults are most likely to spontaneously mention 'Gaining new skills' (17%). Similarly, when prompted, 72% chose this definition."

For each of these words or phrases I read out can you tell me whether you associate it most with a) learning, b) training or c) education?

	Learning	Training	Education	Not stated
	%	%	%	%
Achievement	37	27	34	2
Being taught	31	19	48	3
School	26	3	71	1
Qualifications	12	37	49	2
Gaining new skills	23	72	3	2
Hard work	36	41	18	4
Boring	24	18	31	27
Discovering	70	7	19	3
Enjoyment	62	21	11	6
Computers	30	47	19	4
Finding out more	67	8	21	4
Exchanging ideas	54	16	27	3
Studying	33	7	57	2
TV/Video	60	9	24	8
Personal growth	52	19	23	5

Learners and non-learners

All the most recent research into learning attitudes, including the *National Adult Learning Survey*[8], has found it necessary to differentiate between learners and non-learners. One definition is that a learner is 'someone who has taken part in some kind of learning activity within the last three years'. The key word here seems to be 'activity'. It implies an active searching out

> A learner is someone who has taken part in some kind of learning activity within the last three years

PAGE 13

I am therefore I learn

of learning, a pro-active approach, a positive effort. Yet neither this (nor other more limited definitions) are truly accurate or complete.

The Campaign for Learning has worked hard over the last three years to produce a comprehensive, and comprehensible, definition. Aside from the DfEE/NALS definition mentioned above, they also use the following one, which was commended by the Fryer report[9] last year:

"Learning is a process of active engagement with experience. It is what people do when they want to make sense of the world. It may involve an increase in skills, knowledge or understanding, a deepening of values or the capacity to reflect. Effective learning will lead to change, development and a desire to learn more."

Short of someone hospitalised in a persistent vegetative state, it is hard to conceive of anyone who is a total non-learner. And while it is useful to differentiate between formal and informal learning, between academic and vocational learning and between active and passive learning, it is simply not true to say that anyone is a non-learner in the widest sense.

I am therefore I learn.

Not all learning is 'good' learning. It may, or may not, be useful but is always part of an ongoing process. A child who is continually shouted at or smacked by a parent when it asks questions soon 'learns' not to do so. No one would pretend that this is beneficial but it *is* still learning.

So what this report seeks to address is the barriers to useful, beneficial, developmental learning, and how these barriers might be overcome.

Barriers to Learning

THIS introductory chapter has explored the difference between learning, training and education. It also considered who can be defined as a learner and who as a non-learner.

LEARNING is the broadest of the categories. It is also the term seen, by most survey respondents, in the most positive light. It may involve an increase in skills, knowledge or understanding. Effective learning will lead to change.

EDUCATION is associated with gaining knowledge, usually at a young age. Training is seen as being job- or skill-specific.

A NON-LEARNER, sometimes defined as someone who has undertaken no recent learning activity, is actually a misnomer. If we include informal and passive learning in any definition, then everyone is a learner to some degree – although learning may not always be positive.

SUMMARY of CHAPTER 1

CHAPTER 2

Cultural barriers

BEYOND the individual is the wider community, local and national, our complex, multi-faceted 'society'. This is a mixture of fear and enlightenment, prejudice and reason, shaped by our history and dominated, many would say, by particular national characteristics. This social morass, our 'culture', harbours numerous barriers to learning, which affect both groups and individuals, but which need to be addressed at a national level.

As Malcolm Maguire has written[10], "There is a growing acceptance that it is not sufficient merely to provide training to a certain number of individuals in order to equip them with the skills required to fill identified skill shortage areas. Rather, there has to be a much more fundamental reappraisal of, and attitudinal shift towards, the value attached to learning by society as a whole."

They hate you if you're clever ...

As a nation we are still suspicious of learning, particularly of intellectual or academic excellence. 'Too clever by half' is a put down that does not have a corollary elsewhere in the world. In addition to its work in creating an appetite for learning, the Campaign for Learning has a specific aim to 'change our culture' so that all individuals can learn throughout their life. Look at the verbs – change, create – they imply a *need*, a need to escape from a culture which does *not* value learning as it should, and a need to develop one that does.

Bill Lucas, commenting on the Government's Green Paper, *The Learning Age*, recently wrote[11]: "Let me start by looking at where we are now. It is not a pretty sight. For most of us, learning is something called 'education' for eleven years of our life until the age of 16. Some persist with it until 18. A minority continue into higher education. A few people in other words, do quite well under the present system.

"At work the situation is not much different. There are a few exemplary employee development schemes, and a growing

As a nation we are still suspicious of learning, particularly of intellectual or academic excellence

number of organisations committed to schemes like Investors in People. But their example is not widespread enough. Training at work is, too often, given to those who have already done pretty well out of the education system. If you are at the routine, poorly paid or part-time end of many businesses, then your opportunities to learn will be very limited. We live, in other words, in anything but a learning age at the moment."

The suspicion of learning, and the underlying cultural problem it brings, starts early. In any school today one can still hear the routine 12-year-old's insult aimed at the 'swot' or 'boffin' – someone who works harder or seems more intelligent than the norm – the words sometimes seem charged with a particular vehemence.

... and they despise a fool

While cultural barriers are undoubtedly breaking down, cultural and class stereotypes still exist. As recently as thirty years ago the residual ideas of natural intelligence, inborn ability (or the lack of it) and a social hierarchy were still strong. Their legacy is still with us. That some children are 'brighter' than others (not socially advantaged, better-fed, more stimulated) is still a given in many parts of society.

Cultural barriers ...

> **We still have forms of schooling that reflect a system that was not intended to achieve quality education for all**

The opposite is also true – and the idea of the 'thick' individual of whom school and society has low expectations, persists into early adulthood and beyond. It is perpetuated by individuals themselves, the idea that 'I can't do this or that' starts early and is hard to shift.

Participation in Further, Higher or Adult Education and the desire (or ability) to continue 'learning throughout life' is the continuation of a process which starts at school. Schools reinforce (sometimes unwittingly) social divisions and give children different expectations according to their academic achievement. Though there has been a huge debate and many changes in the last few years, our education system still 'fails' large numbers and once a failure, too often always a failure.

Part of the problem lies with the fact that our education system is still structured, in many ways, towards educating the elite to a high standard but giving the majority only just enough education or training to allow them, if they choose, to be 'productive' members of society. Mel Ainscow wrote[12]: "There is the major problem of how to redesign a system of education that still bears many of the features of the purpose for which it was originally formulated, that of educating those who will take on elite roles in society. It has been argued, for example, that a surgeon from the 19th Century dropped into a present day operating theatre would have no idea where he was, whereas a teacher from that period propelled into a modern day classroom would simply pick up the chalk and carry on where she left off! In other words, despite all the reform efforts of the 20th Century we still have forms of schooling that reflect many of the features of a system that was not intended to achieve quality education for all."

Alan Tuckett reiterated this when he said[13]: "The UK's performance at producing higher-level students is comparable to its competitor nations. However at the lower levels the UK fails to match other countries' ability to produce large numbers of medium-skilled students. Too many students in the UK leave school with low-level or no qualifications."

Should we blame the schools? Is this the root of the problem? It would be easy to do so and many of our less

enlightened politicians do just that. But schools are a mirror of society, not its foundations nor its punch-bag. And there are numerous good schools, the majority of teachers are dedicated, intelligent and committed and there are many examples of learning initiatives that engage and develop pupils in many ways. The present 'Everyone remembers a good teacher' campaign is a timely reminder of this.

The aforementioned MORI poll had this to say about schoolchildren: "Barriers to learning for young people include poor teaching (77%), feeling unhappy (74%) and teachers who do not understand how children learn (72%). Older children are generally more likely to feel that each of the factors has negatively effected their learning, but they are especially likely to feel school and teaching related issues have prevented them from learning. There are few differences between boys and girls, except that girls are more likely to have found learning difficult due to feeling unhappy – 78% to 71%." But there are other factors.

Top of the class

'Class' is a dirty word – one that everybody uses. There is still an enormous class imbalance in 'academic' post-school provision. Though this is being redressed (slowly), FE and HE provision is still dominated by the young, the white, the middle-class and, surprisingly, the male learner. Students from less-favoured backgrounds, whether pertaining to race, class or gender, who do succeed in entering FE and HE institutions, often experience problems and culture conflicts which make them more likely to drop out.

Adult education, whether vocational, academic or hobbyist, is still a middle-class preserve. This is true in many countries, not just the UK. Issues of cost, motivation, time and location are all factors of course but the cultural barrier still seems to exist.

It does not do to be too gloomy here. The problems of participation and access are being recognised and addressed by the current Government. But equally it would be only a complete ostrich that pretended that class differences do not exist.

There is still an enormous class imbalance in academic post-school provision

Cultural barriers ...

Girls are pulling ahead of boys at school

First in the race

If there is a class imbalance in 'academic' post-school provision, there is widespread evidence that people from ethnic minorities feel even more alienated in these white, middle-class learning environments. Racism is still endemic in some sections of our society and it would be fatuous to pretend otherwise. The current public debate over institutionalised racism, whilst not a pretty sight, has been a long time coming.

In spite of (and in some cases because of) attempts to 'multi-culturalise' education, many ethnic minority individuals find some schools and colleges alienating. Add this to other prevalent factors such as language difficulties, lower expectations, family backgrounds where unemployment and low incomes are more common, and a picture of racial inequality begins to emerge. There is also the problem of there being fewer ethnic role models for many groups, whether at the teacher or policy-maker level.

It is dangerous to oversimplify however. There are a huge number of ethnic groups in Britain; this island has historically welcomed and assimilated people from all over the world and continues to do so. Some of the more recent ones may still be in the first throes of 'culture shock' but this is to be expected. Some ethnic groups traditionally have high learning aspirations; others have rarely been encouraged to expect more than the bare minimum. And, in part because of their own cultural norms, women from ethnic minorities tend to get an even rougher deal.

A man's world?

What, then, of gender imbalance and sexism in our society and, particularly, in learning institutions? Recent research suggests that girls are pulling ahead of boys at school – particularly in the younger age groups. More women are now going on to Higher Education and more are in positions of power, authority and influence in society as a whole.

There are still huge gaps of course. In traditionally male-dominated industries and professions there are still few women and this is reflected in their equivalent education

Barriers to Learning

and training feeder systems. There is also, in a (somewhat) gender-biased society, pressure on women not to participate in further education and training. The Campaign for Learning's report *Women's Attitudes to Learning*[14] revealed a degree of personal guilt associated with them learning solely for their own interest. Finally there is still a male agenda in terms of the way teaching and training are conducted. But, on the whole, the male/female area is one where equality of opportunity is increasing and our culture is moving towards parity.

There are still two areas where it is much more difficult for women to partake of learning opportunities. The first is for those with dependent children, particularly single mothers. Many of the problems faced by this group are structural – time, money, childcare – but some are cultural. Though there are some positive developments, most post-16 education and training organisations are not child-friendly – a reflection, perhaps, of our ambivalence as a society towards children. In some sectors of society there is still a widespread cultural perception (amongst men *and* women) that a 'woman's place is in the home'.

Workplace training is a particular problem. Robert Lindley writes[15]: "Women without jobs and with only poor jobs do not have effective access to training. Even when they do, access to continuing career-related training depends on adult and child-care provision to make it possible ... and open occupational structures to make it sustainable."

The 'glass ceiling' is still a reality for many. Reasons vary, but wrong assumptions (often by male managers) about women employees' commitment, capability and ambition is one cause.

Ironically, as Sanderson and Turner point out[16]: "It is a useful rule of thumb that women have the most problems in organisations that claim that women have no problems at all. Equal opportunities are most problematic in organisations that claim that an equal opportunities policy is not necessary because 'We treat everybody equally here'."

The second group of women who, statistically, partake much less in learning opportunities are those from older age groups, whether this is considered to be fifty-plus or somewhat older.

Women
without jobs
often do not
have effective
access to
training

Cultural barriers ...

A civilised society should be measured by how it treats its older members

Old hat?

A recent survey[17] found that nearly one-third of all non-participants in learning activity who say they do not *want* to learn in the future are already 65 and over. Older adults who are active say (like many women) that they learn more for personal satisfaction, self-development purposes and family or leisure reasons than for vocational or work-related ones. This in itself is scarcely surprising. If there are few job opportunities for older people and many no longer want or need to work, then naturally a higher proportion will be uninterested in employment-centred learning.

There are numerous social and economic reasons why 'third age' learning is becoming increasingly important. These are well documented. For example, Tom Schuller has written[18], "The potential of the third age as a source of skill, wisdom and creativity is a huge and immediately available resource. The investment required to tap it is, by comparison, minimal. For once, the long and the short-term coincide."

There are an equal number of social, economic and personal barriers which older people face as they try to come back to or continue with education or training. But are there any cultural ones?

A civilised society is (or should be) measured by how it treats not just its weaker members but its older ones too. And here we fall down rather badly. 'Past it', 'too old', 'over the hill' – age discrimination is rife in western societies.

Employers discriminate against older people and are tacitly encouraged to do so. The images we have of our society, projected by the media, are of a young person's world. Educational institutions are not designed for older people nor do many feel comfortable in them. Many industries are the same. There is a growth in the number of older, formal learners, but it is slower than that in the number of younger ones.

Finally, there is the unspoken perception that investment in learning for older people is economically imprudent. Sadly, this is even evident in the Government's Green Paper, *The Learning Age*. This is related to the fact that, as a society, we still value learning more for the material rewards it can

bring to the individual and the economic benefits to the society than for its own sake.

Cheats and bludgers

Unemployment is a structural barrier to learning, which will be discussed in more detail later, but it is also a cultural issue. The Victorian notion that poverty was entirely the fault of the poor, sloth being the main cause, has been replaced by the widely held view, in some quarters, that unemployment is the fault of the unemployed – that 'they' don't want to work. But 'work' is no longer what it was. Valerie Bayliss, in a recent project report wrote[19]: "In a fluid, uncertain world, asking whether there will be enough jobs to go round will be asking the wrong question, if only because no one will be able to say with certainty, as they have in the past, what a 'job' is."

In spite of the changing nature of work and the fact that the 'job for life' is now, for many, an outdated concept, there is still a real stigma attached to being unemployed. Yet many politicians and economists have accepted in recent years that a certain level of unemployment is both necessary and, in some views, desirable.

If there are barriers to employment then there are barriers to renewing old or learning new skills, for much training is job-related and requires employment for it to be most useful.

If the barriers to learning that face the unemployed (and to a lesser extent the low-skilled) are to be overcome then a good start would be a cultural shift that removes the 'stigma' of unemployment. This would begin to redefine the concept in a similar way to the way in which we need to redefine work.

Down with skool

As has already been suggested, there is an argument that education itself is a divisive agent. One of the characteristics which promotes participation in learning throughout life is social activism – people who participate are already active members of society, and hence already, in the current jargon,

If there are barriers to employment then there are barriers to renewing old or learning new skills

Cultural barriers ...

'empowered stakeholders'. Thus a vicious circle is perpetuated; those who are already well-educated are much more likely to continue with education and training throughout their lives. The figures for those who participate in adult education courses support this. Those who have unpleasant memories of the formal education system, especially those who dropped out early, are less motivated and far less likely to participate in education or training in later life.

The NALS survey found that 'non learners' (i.e. those that had not participated in any learning activity in the last three years) were twice as likely to have left school with no qualifications and to have left full-time education a full two years earlier than 'learners'.

This phenomenon can, in part, be attributed to the class divide, particularly in formal school education, that was mentioned earlier. The OECD's Education Committee report into lifelong learning worldwide in 1996[20] pointed out:

"Among parents there are – depending on the system in question – examples of efforts to maximise the comparative advantage of their own children's education and in so doing ensure that much-needed reforms for the general good cannot take place, or that the learning opportunities available to those who need them most are either inadequate or not available at all."

Usually the effect that parents have on children's learning would be considered under the personal or possibly structural banners. But here is an example of a barrier within the wider 'cultural' picture. Whatever side is taken on the debate on private or grammar schools, home tutors, extra resources paid for by parents and many other related issues, the system, if it needs changing, can clearly only be changed at a macro-political level. And this will only be achieved with great difficulty, in the face of much resistance, over time and possibly at considerable cost.

Writing recently in the Education Guardian[21], a teacher from Northampton commented "It is not the failure of the comprehensive school that leads to national under-achievement – it is because we are not comprehensive enough."

Then there is the academic/vocational divide that our system still perpetuates. There is no doubt that a society that

values NVQs in the same way as it values A levels or higher academic qualifications is still a long way off.

Helena Kennedy wrote recently[22], "Further Education suffers because of prevailing British attitudes. Not only does there remain a very carefully calibrated hierarchy of worthwhile achievement, which has clearly established routes and which privileges academic success well above any other accomplishments, but there is also an appaling ignorance amongst opinion-formers and decision makers about what goes on in Further Education. It is so alien to their experience."

There is a need to look to the future, rather than continue with the system that has served us (more or less) well in the past. The technological age and the changing nature of work are about to place even greater demands on our learning institutions.

Are our education and training systems up to the demands that may be placed on them sooner than we think? It is doubtful. In terms of its philosophy, structures and organisation, our formal education system is rooted in the world of the first industrial revolution. It is essentially still preparing people for a world that is rapidly disappearing. As new challenges arise, people of all ages will need to be competent in a much wider range of existing skills as well as acquiring new ones. If our education system is to cope with 'the knowledge age' a huge cultural shift will be required. Boundaries are becoming blurred also. The skills that people will need to deal with life in general are converging with those they will need for the new world of work.

We are already in a world of 'information overload'. Klas Mellander said not long ago that[23], "We are drowning in information but starving for knowledge." The technologically literate amongst us can access, at the touch of a button, information in quantities that we cannot begin to process efficiently.

Schools, colleges and universities and even the more 'practical' training institutions should be focusing on developing not information transfer but the skills to evaluate and use this information.

Valerie Bayliss[24] has suggested that we need, "To turn the traditional education model on its head. Education should be driven not by examinations that mainly test the memory

> **We can now access information in quantities that we cannot begin to process efficiently**

Cultural barriers ...

but by a new framework of competencies that can be developed through an information base and assessed over time."

Part of the machine

Talking about the future of work and society must not blind us to the current needs and demands that our economic system places on us. At the macro level, a financial system which demands quick returns for shareholders mitigates against leaders of industry investing in the long-term – and thus in learning.

The pressure to 'get a job' has its corollary 'gain the skills that make you employable'. Industry calls the tune. From schoolchildren to graduates, there is an ever-increasing pressure to be 'employable'. In the world of training this has been known for years of course. All vocational training, from low level skills to high-level management development is designed to help the individual achieve employment, stay in work, get promotion or move to a better job.

Education/business partnerships are an excellent concept with much to recommend them. But there is a downside. Education institutions are becoming geared to the needs of business, sometimes to the detriment of more abstract 'learning'. Industry may pay lip service to wanting creative, flexible people with transferable skills and open minds. What they all too often really want are malleable clones who will fit into a pre-packaged company ethos.

Then there is the ever-increasing demand for paper qualifications. A recent study in Holland[25] found a syndrome (also applicable to many other developed countries) which is proving to be an 'inverse' barrier. Dutch people are finding it increasingly difficult to gain employment to match their educational qualifications, even though jobs require ever-higher standards. The rush for diplomas and certificates has resulted in the standard of employee qualifications rising even faster than jobs require, a syndrome familiar in Britain and America as the 'Diploma Disease'.

The hardest hit are, as usual, people with little or no qualifications, more highly educated employees are replacing them in their jobs. A 1998 study called *"Over-educated"*

shows that three years ago 38% of the working population had a job below the level to which they had been educated. Twenty-five years ago this was only 17%. This trend can be seen throughout the employment spectrum, which creates a downward spiral, pushing aside those less educated.

Will there be a backlash with people saying, "There's no point in me continuing to study if the goalposts keep shifting?"

Job, what job?

There is not the space here, nor is it the purpose of this guide, to discuss in detail the wider economic conditions that impact on attitudes to learning and the desire to learn. However, mention must be made of the changing economic circumstances which affect a proportion of the most vulnerable people in society and crosses over into structural (economic) barriers to learning and personal (motivational) ones. The situation was well summed up in 1998 in a speech by Elaine Applebee[26].

"The departure of 'work' from 'working class' communities has affected not only the local economy but also the culture of family and society. The cultural glue, which gives meaning to every area of life, bonding people to one another, is rapidly dissolving.

"An example of this is what has happened to the socialisation of young men in such communities. Work provided an important support to parents as their teenagers grew to be men. It provided the means by which young, daft boys became sensible young men to whom young women were prepared to commit themselves (and we see the knock-on effect on family structure where men tend to be absent). The workplace provided older men and a hierarchy through which boys learnt skills, discipline and self-control. When the paid work disappeared, so did the contribution it made to this process.

"The workplace also provided other sorts of learning. Apprenticeships, often with day release to college, kept young people within a self-conscious learning environment until the age of twenty-one. Trades Union involvement provided a place where skills in organisation and participation

The departure of 'work' from 'working class' has affected the culture of family and society

Cultural barriers ...

The loss of work has meant the loss of much else, not least learning opportunities

could be developed and a live encounter with democracy could happen. People learnt that whilst they might not have the power and influence of those higher up the social scale, by working together with others they could create their own comparative power base from which they could attempt to influence the course of their lives."

Mention could also be made of the increased leisure opportunities that work gave and how informal learning flourished. Friendships formed at work were carried out into the community and created wider networks of association. The loss of work has meant the loss of much else, not least learning opportunities.

For those children being brought up in a household where no-one works, these opportunities may never come again. Schools, industry and politicians do have to be careful therefore not to alienate them further with the message that education is solely about paid work.

Lip service

There seems to be general agreement among policy makers, industrialists, worker representatives, educators, and most individuals on the need to create (or further develop) a learning culture across all sectors of society. In the words of Christopher Ball[27], "Learning pays – nothing much else does."

Yet the record, particularly in business, in moving towards this desired state of affairs is patchy. In tough economic times it is still, all too often, an organisation's training budget that is among the first elements to be cut back.

For every manager who sees the development of people as being on a par with, if not more important than, product improvement, marketing or cost efficiency, there is another who sees people simply as economic cannon fodder. While quality may be improving in many areas, and training budgets increasing in some companies and sectors, the quantity of in-work training is in decline. The link between highly trained and continuously developing employees and economic success (however measured) is still not sufficiently widely recognised.

Barriers to Learning

Better the devil you know

The 'learning organisation', like the learning society, is another concept 'honoured more in the breach than the observance'. There are some organisations where learning is valued, but there are many more where it is treated with suspicion or even hostility.

Most of our larger corporations, public as well as private, are still modelled on the 18th and 19th Century principles of a hierarchical 'command and control' structure. Those who, rightly, demand a shift to more open, flatter, flexible structures have to recognise that they are struggling against a huge cultural barrier – one built up over many years. The point about the way in which these organisations worked is that it was stable and efficient and thus still has a large number of defenders. Change may be necessary but major change is also frightening.

On a societal level, threatening the status quo is equally difficult and time consuming. On the one hand are those who are suspicious of, and resistant to, all forms of change. If it is hard to shift attitudes at an individual level (and it is) then at a societal level it is exponentially greater.

There is a small but vocal movement that is questioning the very assumption that we should be developing a 'learning' society. The Economic and Social Research Council takes a swipe at some commonplaces such as 'the firm that learns wins', 'work now demands a fusion of thinking and doing and learning', 'survival in conditions of global competition depends on continuous re-skilling', 'a new social divide is opening between the trained and the untrained'. The Council suggests that we need to be wary of the 'common sense' view that more skills are necessarily better and goes on to question the whole area of vocational training and qualifications[28].

Then there is a diminishing but still loud voice that asks whether creating an appetite to learn amongst all members of society might not have a destabilising effect upon it. This can perhaps be best illustrated by the situation in many developing countries where the pressure for social change, even revolution, is most often led by students or other members

> Creating an appetite to learn amongst all members of society might have a destabilising effect

Cultural barriers ...

Why spend money training staff so that they can move to another job taking their new skills with them?

of an educational elite. The growth of the Internet is causing concern at a political/state level in many countries where the flow of information has, until now, been tightly controlled.

Last year Frank Coffield[29] flagged up a growing mistrust of the 'evangelical fervour' of the proponents of learning: "One challenge is to confront the argument that, behind the benevolent intentions and the high flown rhetoric, lifelong learning, the learning society and the learning organisation are all being propounded to induce individuals to become more-or-less willing participants in learning for life and to bear an increasing proportion of the costs of such learning without end. In the sense that society always employs a variety of social processes to ensure that its members conform to its changing expectations, lifelong learning is viewed by some as the latest form of social control."

The real value of this approach is that it breaks the cosy consensus on lifelong learning in the UK and may even provoke some much needed controversy and debate on the topic.

In many western countries, mistrust is shown in microcosm at company level where there is often a resistance by those in positions of power to the empowerment (read education, training or learning) of subordinates. Some companies, indeed some public sector organisations, have a culture which fears development. "The more people are trained the more likely they are to covet my job," thinks the senior manager. "The more people are trained, the more likely they are to head for (better paid) pastures new," says the Head of Personnel.

Jacqui Linton wrote not long ago[30]: "An all too common belief held by many organisations is 'Why spend all that money training staff so that they can move to another job taking their newly acquired skills with them'." This syndrome will be explored more fully in the following 'structural' chapter.

Jam today

Is there the political will to make the changes necessary to bring about a learning society? Education and lifetime learning may be at the forefront of policy making at the

moment but will the, necessarily long-term, strategies needed survive other short-term imperatives? This question is especially pertinent in the light of an economic slowdown. Other priorities may get in the way of the investment required.

The nature of our political system, and that of most other countries, has meant that changes in political leadership have undermined changes in our learning organisations in the past and may well do so in the future. If there is the possibility of much of the debate around learning being taken out of the political arena or at least taken to one remove then the chances for a consistent long-term strategy being implemented are much greater.

Two years ago, in a speech at Ruskin College, Tony Blair seemed to offer a fairly large olive branch to warring factions when he said, "I believe there is the chance to forge a new consensus on education policy. It will be practical not ideological. *And it will put behind us the political and ideological debates that have dominated the last thirty years.* The foundations of the consensus are clear. Early support for children under the age of five. Primary schools delivering high standards of literacy and numeracy. Rigorous assessment of pupil and school performance, and action based upon it. Improved training and qualifications for teachers, especially head-teachers. Early intervention when things go wrong. Support from all sections of the community to ensure that all our children are given the best possible start. And we must never forget that education is not a one-off event for the under 18s. The new consensus must be based on wide access to higher education and continual opportunities for all adults to learn throughout life."

Yet although there may be some movement to consensus behind the scenes, the old adversarial standards still apply – as the recent debate on grammar schools shows.

Free will

Another strand of our culture that makes the development of a learning society more problematical is the libertarian attitude that says that all decisions should be left to the individual – who should then take the consequences. This

> **There is the chance to forge a new consensus on education policy that will be practical not ideological**

Cultural barriers ...

Adults should be allowed to remain less literate, less competent and less cultured if they wish

manifests itself strongly in our national suspicion of, and resistance to, any form of coercion. This provides us, at a cultural level, with a moral dilemma. Is it acceptable to choose not to learn?

Naomi Sargant wrote[31]: "There remains the moral issue of whether educators should actively intervene to persuade non-participants to learn. Some would argue that provided people are aware of opportunities, and the opportunities are accessible, enough is being done. Adults should be allowed to make their own decisions, remaining less 'literate', less 'competent', less 'cultured' if they wish, and to spend their time on other things if that is what they prefer to do. The attitude equates with the sentiment 'you can take a horse to water but you cannot make it drink'."

There are also those in our society (a small but perhaps growing number) who do not trust the quality of the afore-mentioned 'water'. This group has what may be termed 'an alternative social vision' and rejects many of our current social and economic norms (for example the idea that economic growth is intrinsically worthwhile) and with this rejects or distrusts our formal education system.

And finally

Making a cultural shift towards a learning society is much harder than many commentators or policy makers recognise.

At a Campaign for Learning colloquium a couple of years ago, American writer and educationalist, Geoffrey Caine, made the point that, in earlier civilisations, schooling aimed to perpetuate the past (or at least the status quo). The same, to some degree, was true of further education and, particularly, work-based training. Our needs today are for learning that will help us move towards a new and more complex future.

We exist in a culture that is locked into the past more closely than many of us will admit. This may prove to be one of the biggest barriers of all.

Barriers to Learning

Main cultural barriers explored in this chapter:
- National attitudes
- National characteristics
- Division by:
    Class
    Ethnic origin
    Gender
    Age
- Industry needs & pressures
- Lack of leadership
- Threats to social status quo
- Cultural/media pressure
- Political priorities and changing strategy
- Lack of industry/education co-operation
- Freedom, morality and 'libertarian' views
- Disempowerment & alienation
- Firm vs individual needs
- Learning vs training
- Academic/vocational divide

Cultural barriers ...

MOST policy statements, from different sources, recognise the need for a cultural shift so that all individuals can learn throughout their life. The implication is that we do not have a 'learning society' at present.

CULTURAL barriers to learning include those relating to class, ethnic origin, gender and age. Unemployment carries a cultural stigma that can impact upon active learning.

THOSE who are already well-educated are much more likely to continue with education and training throughout their lives. Under-achievers at school are far less likely to be life-long learners.

THE short term needs of business also present barriers and some education institutions are finding this can affect learning in a number of ways. At a national policy level too, short-termism and the adversarial nature of our political system can hinder the development of an effective learning strategy.

OUR education system is rooted in an economic and social philosophy that was designed for a different industrial era. There is still too much emphasis on information transfer rather than 'finding out'.

THERE is still a significant academic/vocational divide with vocational qualifications perceived as having a lower value. Past attitudes manifest this and other cultural barriers, and are slow to change.

THERE is also some debate over whether it is right for anyone to choose not to learn or for the state to actively intervene to promote adult learning – should there not simply be freedom of choice?

CHAPTER 3

Structural barriers

WE HAVE seen that there are barriers to learning at the 'macro' or cultural level, the removal or diminishing of which will take a change of national attitudes to learning and many other related subjects. It will also involve much effort and commitment, a certain amount of money and, above all, time.

Sometime, never

A lack of time to engage in (especially formal) learning is often quoted by respondents to surveys as one of the biggest barriers to learning. Once compulsory education is completed (i.e. at the age of 16) all learning is voluntary to a greater or lesser degree. Even with work-related training or the continuation of education there is always the opportunity for the learner to refuse to attend or participate.

A lack of time *per se* is not an applicable barrier when applied to those in formal, structured learning, notably young people. If a learner is in full-time pre-16 education then that is *all* they have to do (apart from meeting obvious basic needs – food, sleep etc). Equally, the elderly, who face many barriers, do not have a time problem.

The time factor is most often cited as a barrier by two specific groups – those in work and those with caring responsibilities.

Workers have pressing demands on their time, which naturally limit opportunities for learning. Jobs have to be done – or companies fail and individuals don't get paid. That much is obvious. There has also been much discussion in the latter part of the 90's of how work pressures are increasing. In an attempt to increase efficiency, maximise profit or, in some cases, simply to survive in a highly competitive environment, organisations are asking or demanding more from their workers. The 'delayering' of organisations, for example, has meant that whole swathes of (usually middle) management have been removed, leaving the remainder to do more work. The increasing trend to company mergers has had a similar effect. It is probably the case that this increased pressure has

Lack of time is seen as one of the biggest barriers to learning

Part-time workers miss out on training opportunities

had three related effects on learning: first there is simply less time for formal training, secondly there is less time for informal learning, and third there is less motivation, on the part of somewhat demoralised staff, to undertake learning activities.

While managers and other employees in large organisations grapple with these restrictions and pressures on their time, those in smaller businesses suffer even greater problems. At the worker/producer level in a small company, time off for training can often directly equate to lost business or production. And at the management level (and in very small companies the management/worker distinction is often non-existent) time off for training can equally mean lost business or opportunities.

Bob Wilson, a management consultant, who spent thirty years working with small companies, found that their 'time-related' problems were two-fold: "Small firms face a number of barriers that either stop training 'dead in its tracks' or dilute its impact. Commonly, these are a 'seat of the pants' approach to training and workforce skills which means that problems are only identified when they reach near-crisis point and are then solved with short-term measures, or a skewed 'task' culture, in which production or operations targets are emphasised to the exclusion of training and development."

If owners, managers and workers in small companies have a difficulty with finding time for training, this problem is especially acute when a worker is temporary or part-time. Part-time workers often have low-skilled jobs and work unsocial hours when training is not available. They may have more than one part-time job, further restricting the time available for training.

Temporary workers are often left outside the company culture – thereby missing such training as may be available. They may also face reluctance on the part of the employer to train them. Ironically, they may find that when a period of employment finishes and they do have the time to upgrade their skills, the opportunity to do so is no longer there.

The most common time restriction on part-time, casual and temporary workers is that they are likely to have other important commitments. These are most likely to be family or caring responsibilities. Unsurprisingly, research has

Barriers to Learning

shown[32] this to be particularly true of women, and especially single mothers[33]. This is a group that faces many barriers to learning in addition to a lack of time – these will be discussed later.

Job hunters might be expected to have more time than most to undertake skills training or personal development. However, there are still benefit rules in the UK which militate against them doing so. The system considers, quite unrealistically, that any time that is not directly put in to active job-seeking is time wasted. The benefit rules that reflect this will be considered later.

Some researchers are highly suspicious of the 'excuse' that 'lack of time' is a real reason why people will not or cannot undertake learning activity. It is true that work demands or family caring responsibilities, given as reasons, can mask more fundamental barriers – such as a lack of motivation. However, as we have seen, amongst certain groups the time factor is a key obstacle.

A few respondents to surveys will admit that they believe they 'have better things to do with their time' than undertake learning. It is likely that many more have (or feel they have) alternative priorities for the use of leisure time. This is part of the low priority that many individuals give to learning and brings us back to an overarching 'cultural' barrier.

Structural barriers ...

Money, money, money

Learning pays, of course it does, but it also costs. One of the first questions that anyone approaching education or training, from whatever standpoint, will want answered is, "How much will it cost?" This question is as likely to be asked by a parent faced with an extra-curricular school activity, an employer considering a training programme for staff, a pensioner thinking about an adult education course or a College Principal faced with a Government directive to increase student numbers.

The fact is that learning costs money – and someone, somewhere has to pay the piper. We have already observed that some employers are reluctant to fund training for a variety of reasons, such as having more important priorities, lack of perceived value and the fear that trained employees may leave. However many, if not most, employers do spend a proportion of their budgets on work-related training, and the more enlightened also contribute funds to employee development schemes.

For those adults who do not have access to employer-provided training and wish to increase their skills or aspire to further education, there are a number of financial problems. The first is, of course, the actual cost of the learning. A percentage, sometimes the whole, of tuition fees at all Higher Education establishments and most FE ones now have to be borne by the learner. In some cases, over a two or three-year course, this can run into thousands of pounds. A 1999 University guide[34] observes that some current graduates are leaving with as much as £10,000 worth of debt hanging over them. Rent rises, tuition fee payments and discrepancies between HE establishments mean that this figure could rise to £15,000 for some of those currently studying. It is hardly surprising then that the drop-out rate at some universities now stands at an average of 19%, with one reporting a rate of nearly 40%.

A survey[35] of young people's attitudes to FE found that there was now a strong perception of a lack of financial support for further and higher education students. This was heavily criticised by young people. Some were put off continuing in education by the prospect of poverty and the stress of having to work to support themselves while studying full time. 55% of 12-25 year olds said that young people don't go into further education because they can't afford to (45% of 12-15 year olds rising to 72% of 22-25 year olds).

And, as usual, those from better-off backgrounds have a head start. One of our newer universities recently responded to the Higher Education Commission thus: "The system continues to benefit differentially those coming from the most wealthy households and uniform eligibility for 'cheap' loans continues to do so to some extent."

Shorter courses from colleges, private providers, industry skill centres and the like, all have fee structures which require money from the individual in many, if not most, cases. But often more important to the individual are the many 'extra' costs that education or training courses carry. Examples of these include travel, dependent care, books and equipment, clothing, tools and exam or certification fees.

And more money

An equal problem for many individuals is the below-the-line cost of undertaking formal learning. Courses may require a time commitment that involves a loss of income. For the unemployed a loss of benefit may sometimes accrue from them taking a course (benefit rules have been relaxed recently but there are still anomalies which present a financial barrier to training). The family situation, where one partner resents limited money being spent on skills training for the other, is not uncommon; nearly all research has found that women, especially, place family 'needs' above their own desire for learning[36].

Where course fees are payable in advance, as is often the case, individuals may simply not be able to raise a sufficient lump sum. Many people have a reluctance to borrow money in such situations and often borrowing, where there is no security available, is prohibitively expensive.

As the desire and the need for learning increases – and if we are truly building a learning society this will continue – the sheer pressure of numbers requiring financial assistance puts pressure on funding bodies. The cupboard is frequently

The university system continues to benefit differentially those coming from the most wealthy households

Structural barriers ...

The learning cake needs to be enlarged

bare. Some local authorities, for example, are cutting the funding on offer or shifting the emphasis so that only statutory requirements are being met.

Finally, there is the 'half a loaf' syndrome. Financial constraints may not eliminate learning opportunities but may mean that inappropriate cheaper courses are chosen by those with a burning commitment to learn rather than longer or more expensive ones.

It is not just individuals who feel financial pressure. Learning providers operate in an increasingly complex and highly regulated environment. Work-related training is now almost entirely funded on an 'outcome' basis; no qualification, job or other 'positive' outcome – no money. Courses are filled with those who are judged to be likely to complete them and succeed – meaning that training for those who perhaps need it most becomes more limited. Obstacles also appear in the form of unresponsive and inflexible funding regimes and continual, politically motivated, changes to funding structures.

Then there is the pressure of numbers. There has been a vast increase in the number of those moving from school to FE (partly as a result of fewer low-skill job opportunities and benefit changes for 16 and 17 year-olds). There has not, FE colleges argue, been a concomitant increase in funding. Dick Evans wrote recently[37], "Many colleges are experimenting, out of economic necessity, with attempting to produce quality of performance which satisfies the student, at the lowest possible cost to the organisation." There is a tension here and inevitably sometimes quality suffers and dissatisfaction increases.

At a national level more money is being spent on education and training than ever before. Yet everyone involved, head-teachers, college lecturers, private training companies, TECs, NTOs, LEAs, Adult Education organisations, special-needs groups, minority providers and even industry, continue to press for a bigger slice of the learning cake or for the cake itself to be enlarged.

More money in itself will not solve all problems. There are far too many funding anomalies in our system at present. Things have not changed much since eight years ago when

Barriers to Learning

Veronica McGivney wrote: "Entitlement to financial support varies widely according to a person's place of residence, the type and level of course taken, and mode of attendance. LEAs differ enormously in their treatment of adult learners and there is little coherence in concessionary fee structures for part-time students or recoupment arrangements. Variations in fee levels and complicated arrangements for different categories of student lead to confusion and resentment and may deter potential students." At the time of writing, it is still the case that student loans are not available for anyone over the age of 50.

It is not just a question of the *amount* of funding available nationally. Better targeting is required. Bob Fryer commented last year[38], "One especially frustrating obstacle (for the learner) is the sudden withdrawal of small, but crucial, amounts of funding or support for projects which have begun to draw people in, build up their enthusiasm and produce positive results. The loss of support might come because of the end of short-term funding, because so-called 'matched' funding cannot be raised or because the marginal costs of continuing funding are deemed to be too great for the college or local authority which previously gave support. It might simply be that the project fell within a group of activities cut at a time of spending restrictions ... Whatever the cause, the consequences are often disastrous for the learners involved and for their morale. At best, it confirms the suspicions of those who already believe their interests are not a prime concern of those in authority. At worst, it reinforces hostility to education and cynicism towards those who advocate it as one aspect of enhanced citizenship."

There is a 'reverse' issue that needs to be aired here. Financial help for any learning project, whether from the State or from other sources, can have a negative impact on the participant. This is an argument that is trotted out whenever an authority wishes to cut funding and so must be treated with great care. However it does seem generally true that once a commitment has been made by an individual to contribute financially to his or her own development, then there is more likelihood of completion and more sense of ownership. A recent large research study[39] into student

Better targeting of funding is needed

The lack of affordable, available childcare prevents many women from taking up education or training opportunities

drop-out rates in the UK found an interesting correlation between whether the individual was or was not responsible for paying their fees and course completion. 90% of those who left courses early were paying no fees or paying at reduced levels. Those who pay their own fees have, it is therefore argued, a greater commitment and desire to complete and succeed in their chosen area.

One final caveat on funding. As with 'time' barriers to learning, it is important to recognise financial barriers but not to overstate them. 'I can't afford it,' often masks a deeper reason for non-participation.

Who cares?

The Daycare Trust wrote, two years ago[40]: "In the UK today, there is a massive gap between the childcare services families need and the childcare services that exist. Children are missing out on quality childcare either because they live in an area where it does not exist or because their families cannot afford to pay for it. Parents are missing out on the chance to work or study because they can't find childcare they can afford. Others are making do with unstable arrangements or confining themselves to jobs that fit in around school hours or evenings and are often badly paid. There is a growing polarisation between work rich and work poor families."

Most of the debate around childcare provision has centred on the need for women, especially single mothers, to return to, or start, work. But the lack of affordable, available childcare also prevents many women from taking up education or training opportunities. The 'childcare problem' is, for some, at the root of three barriers to learning mentioned in this chapter. All too often the problem of cost is directly related to the need to pay for childcare. Equally the problem of time is often related to the need to be at home for a good proportion of the training week. Finally there is the problem of flexibility. As we shall see later, many courses of training or further education are aimed at those with no other commitments. Part-time, modular and above all *flexible* training arrangements are simply not available.

In 1995 there were nearly six million children under the

age of eight in Britain but less than 700,000 registered child-care places. There was only one childcare place for every nine children under eight.

Childcare services are not evenly distributed across the country. Instead there is a fragmented patchwork of services depending upon local income levels, local authority policies and the socio-economic history of an area.

Work and learning are intricately intertwined here. Childcare arrangements for one need are as likely to be as bad (or as good) as for the other. But if care arrangements are inadequate for either then the motivation to move from unemployment, through learning, and into work, is much lower. Even where childcare arrangements are provided by a learning institution, the learner may find that these are not available at the right time, and are not repeated in the big bad world of work afterwards.

Whilst the childcare situation is improving slowly, especially with the development of the National Childcare Strategy, it will be a long time before affordable arrangements put learning within the reach of a large proportion of women and even some men.

Where do you go to?

Child care provision is just one aspect of how where you live or work can have a significant effect on your opportunity for learning. We have already discussed how different local authorities offer different levels of financial support across the UK.

Learning is not provided on an equal or equitable basis either. We find schools that are vastly different in terms of quality of provision, facilities, equipment, culture and perhaps most importantly, expectations. Even the best teachers, if they have a high proportion of special needs, disruptive or second-language children may spend more time on remedial work or 'crowd control' than the curriculum allows for.

But if, in some areas, learning provision is much poorer than in others, there are some where there is no provision at all. Take the example of the company that refuses to or cannot afford to train its personnel. What should those who are

Schools are vastly different in terms of quality of provision, facilities, equipment, culture and expectations

Structural barriers ...

Some courses are designed to be economic for the provider rather than accessible to the learner

keen to develop new skills do? The glib answer to this is that people can always change to a 'better' employer, find the money and time to study outside the work environment, persuade their union to include skills bargaining in its negotiations, open communication channels with the employer to change the company culture – all worthy solutions. But some of these, indeed often all of them, are not always possible. Regional imbalances in training provision are as widespread as they are in education.

Then there is travel. This may be just another cost barrier but in some cases it is simply an, often insurmountable, barrier in its own right. Not everyone in 'our great car economy' has a private car. The young, the elderly, the poor, many of the disabled depend on other forms of transport. But public transport is patchy to say the least. Buses simply do not run regularly any longer in vast swathes of rural Britain. Rail travel is expensive and becoming (at least to the layman's eyes) progressively less widespread. Taxis are prohibitively costly. In many regions, even urban areas, public transport ceases at night. You may be able to get to an evening course at seven in the evening only to find there is no way home again at nine-thirty.

Where there is reasonable formal learning provision then courses are frequently organised at inappropriate times and in inaccessible places – designed to be economic for the provider rather than accessible to the learner. Even within a learning environment this problem of access, location and time can surface. How often are school or college timetables devised with the needs of teachers and administrators in mind rather than those of the learners? It is easy to suspect the answer is 'almost always'.

A full-time worker may or may not have access to training at work. A part-timer will have concomitantly less. Surveys suggest that many employers have an unconscious bias against providing opportunities for part-timers as they are often valued less. Opportunities outside work may be even more limited. Those who work part-time or who have other commitments that affect their availability for learning find that far too many courses are not delivered on a part-time basis.

FE Colleges provide both academic and work-related

courses, so it is instructive to look at how their provision is geared to the needs of learners and potential learners.

Most provision is still full time. Most learners are young, with few or no family commitments and provided with some (if not sufficient) funding. Provision for adults, returners, the elderly, the unemployed, those who can only study part-time and even those whose learning styles or preferences do not fit with the type of provision – all are marginalised. Yet school stops at 16. Higher Education is still an unattainable mountain peak for most learners. Private training providers are declining in number, and in the range of courses they provide. Adult education classes are being cut in many areas and have a cost involved that puts them out of the reach of many. Many companies tend to train only full-time workers, some restrict training to very narrow areas and some do not train at all.

All the money, all the time, all the motivation in the world will not help you if the learning provision is simply *not there*.

Pointing the way

In spite of the problems that learners face in terms of money, time and access, there is a lot of high quality learning provision available. But, as we have already noted, take-up by those who most *need* to learn (the currently disadvantaged) is low.

There are many reasons for this but one of the main ones is that they simply *do not know* what opportunities are available. And even when they are given good, impartial information there is little evidence that this, in itself, leads to increased take-up.

Broadly, the evidence shows that guidance for young people still at school is quite adequate. Choices between continuing in education, taking up more vocational or work-related training, moving into employment or self-employment, taking time out for reflection and self-development are offered on a reasonably well-structured basis. The only major problem with impartiality comes when fifteen or sixteen year-olds are persuaded to stay on into the 6th form for reasons that have to do more with financial benefits to the school than academic ones to the pupil.

The take-up by those who most need to learn is low

Structural barriers ...

In many large organisations, there is also a clear and well-developed guidance system. But there are many individuals who fall outside these two categories including those who most need assistance.

There is currently no coherent national strategy on adult guidance. With the launch of *Learning Direct*, the DfEE funded free-phone information and advice line for learning opportunities, now taken under the wing of the University for Industry, this may be partially addressed in the near future. But many people are unsure of where to go for guidance and far from certain that if they do find it that the guidance will be relevant, appropriate and impartial.

Two years ago Andrea Spurling wrote[41]: "It is largely a matter of chance whether adults can find good guidance when they need it. There is no easily recognisable nation-wide system of quality assurance to show that adult guidance in different situations conforms to a common set of standards centred on the individual's needs."

If guidance for adults in general is 'patchy', then for two particular groups it is worse than that.

For those who are currently unemployed, 'guidance' is often tied to national policy (on for example re-skilling in certain areas or reducing unemployment figures). Benefit entitlement may be affected by the individual's decision as to whether to apply for a particular job or begin a specific training scheme. Guidance is often, though not always, affected by factors other than the most appropriate route for the individual to take.

This situation has led to a distrust of some guidance and advice systems and to a large minority of disaffected adults who feel marginalised or exploited. A bad experience of guidance can easily kill off any desire to start or continue learning at an early stage. And then there is the fact that most people only look for advice or guidance on learning, and particularly on career development, at times of crisis. Unemployment or the threat of redundancy, with all its attendant stress, is not the best time to be calmly considering which path through life to follow.

Finally there is much debate about the funding of guidance. If there is to be a comprehensive adult guidance system,

with a national structure and mission but delivered on a local basis, then who is to pay for it? Effective, sympathetic and extensive guidance for all will be expensive. And effective delivery of this guidance on the ground may prove even more so.

Out of the loop

Guidance, finance, travel and many other barriers can be particularly acute for the unemployed. As was observed in the 'cultural' section of this report there is something of a vicious circle at work here. As skill requirements rise there is the 'no training – no job, no job – no training' dichotomy.

In spite of the plethora of Government training 'schemes' over the last 20 years, some successful, some less so, it remains the case that the unemployed, particularly the long-term jobless, have less access to learning opportunities than those in work. Figures regularly confirm this – in 1998 an Institute for Fiscal Studies report found that 14% of those without qualifications were unemployed, compared to only 7% of those with degrees or higher level vocational qualifications.

Unemployment might be expected to act as a stimulus to seeking increased skill levels but often it is a deterrent. There are also other factors at work and there is not always a clear link between unemployment and lack of education and training. Some of the reasons for long-term unemployment have been identified as:

• Industrial factors – shift from manufacturing to service economy, decline in old industrial areas
• Geographical factors
• Family commitments – childcare problems and the need to support other dependent relatives
• Age problems – resistance to accepting older adults on training courses and in employment
• Health or disablement problems

A lack of training and education is not necessarily a direct cause or consequence of these and they are not therefore always susceptible to a 'learning solution'; changes in social policy and, perhaps, employer attitudes are also needed.

No training – no job, no job – no training

Structural barriers ...

The local education and training 'market' is a complete jungle

There are some interesting developments taking place on both cultural and structural levels to overcome the 'problem of unemployment'. Certainly it is not for want of discussion or policy initiatives that a learning problem still exists. There is also a further factor; unemployment, over time, saps motivation – either to find a job or to retrain. This is a 'personal' barrier and will be explored more fully in the next chapter.

Too much, too young

The fact that we are 'drowning in information' is nowhere more clearly seen than in the range of establishments competing to provide education and training.

In London, a group of young people, of the same age and from the same comprehensive school, is being monitored as they move from their last year at school into the world of work, further education, joblessness and schemes[42]. This local education and training 'market' is a complete jungle.

In their particular local area there are sixteen providers of courses: FE, sixth form and tertiary colleges and courses provided under the auspices of the local TEC. Some young people are going on through A Level into higher education, some into training, some into work, some onto the New Deal, and some, who have already effectively left school before the age of 16, are existing in the 'grey' economy.

At the same time these young people are required to grasp the extraordinary plethora of qualifications that they can attempt post-GCSE. There are over 30,000 qualifications that can now be taken in FE colleges.

Those involved professionally in education and training may find it difficult to understand just how confusing this can be. In 1986 the National Council for Vocational Qualifications (NCVQ) was set up to 'rationalise' the situation and this was further developed in 1997 with the merger with the Schools Curriculum and Assessment Authority (SCAA) and the setting up of the Qualifications and Curriculum Authority (QCA). But in 1999 we still have:
• Degrees (first and further)
• A levels
• A/S levels

Barriers to Learning

- GNVQs
- NVQs (and their Scottish equivalents)
- Access courses
- ONDs
- HNDs
- City & Guilds qualifications
- BTEC qualifications
- Key skills qualifications
- A range of professional qualifications
- A range of management qualifications
- Further industry-related qualifications
- Sports & leisure qualifications
- And numerous others.

Attempts to make the system simpler have failed – and not necessarily for negative reasons. Transferable qualifications, modular courses, open credits, 'bite-sized chunks of learning', make achieving tangible results easier for some, even when the terminology confuses others. David Pardey, writing on management qualifications[43], but with application to most other vocational qualifications, said:

"The expectation of both the government and NCVQ (in 1986) was that competence-based qualifications would systematically replace all the existing vocational awards until only National Vocational Qualifications (NVQ) and Scottish Vocational Qualifications (SVQ) were left.

"Why didn't it happen? The simple answer is that the market wouldn't let it. The qualifications system in the UK has developed over many decades in response to the demand from employers and employees. Despite criticism from many quarters that the existing qualifications system was too inflexible, unrelated to the actual workplace and had the effect of restricting access, when the new S/NVQs became available it was clear that for many the existing awards were both highly valued and wanted."

The Campaign for Learning's 1998 MORI poll asked about qualifications and had this to say: "The perceived emphasis placed on obtaining qualifications is a barrier to some peoples' involvement in learning. A large majority (37%) of adults says the stress laid on qualifications has put

A large majority of adults says the stress laid on qualifications has put them off learning

Structural barriers ...

The use of
acronyms and
jargon can be
a barrier

them off learning. Younger people and those without qualifications are particularly likely to mention this."

Speaking in tongues

Then there is the (sometimes seemingly deliberate) use of jargon and acronyms and obscure 'academic speak' to confuse the young person (or adult) further.

In the Fryer report[44], it was stated: "Barriers include the confusing multiplicity of acronyms and jargon and the existence of a whole vocabulary which is itself off-putting and damaging to fragile and tentative motivation ... seen from the point of view of those potential learners whom we seek to motivate, the situation can easily appear confusing, intimidating and clear confirmation that 'education is for other people' who appear to be able to find their way through the maze."

Once again it is those that most need to be brought back into a learning environment who are most likely to be daunted at the maze's gateway.

As an example of 'off-putting' language, used by academics, try this:

"Consequently, while attempting to regulate and standardise the evaluation of education placements, there has been an emphasis on the requirement of those decision-makers on the success or otherwise of the placement to validate their judgements. Thus, such evaluations are overly-permeated with empirical, 'scientific' objectivity – positivism re-born."

The tendency of learning professionals to talk in a language that excludes the lay person is widespread.

How about this? "These problems also point to weaknesses in the methodologies used to develop vocational qualifications. The favoured approach has been functional analysis which essentially involves deciding on the key purpose of an occupation and then disaggregating it into subsidiary functions until an assessable level of detail is reached."

The second example was from someone trying to de-mystify NVQs!

Then there is the plethora of acronyms and initials used in the learning world. NVQ is a clumsy acronym, APL is

another, GNVQ even more so. Many people still think that a TEC is the local technical college. Ask the average small business person to differentiate between IiP, ILAs, the IES and the IPPR; or the NCVQ, the NCVO and the NCITO. A blank look is the likely response.

The good, the bad and ...

As we have seen, educationalists, trainers, and, to a lesser extent teachers, sometimes build barriers through the use of jargon, acronyms or the plethora of qualifications; but there is a deeper problem which can put people off not just learning throughout life but off learning *for* life.

If families are the foundation of education, as is discussed in the next chapter, the first structure to be built on these foundations is in the control of primary and secondary teachers. Good teachers abound. But there are, unfortunately, still a number who are less good and a few who are downright bad. Just as most of us remember the inspiring teachers who instilled the love of a particular subject (which can last a lifetime) so, equally, most of us will remember the poor teacher who 'put us off' a subject – again quite possibly for life. For every Robin Williams character in *'Dead Poets Society'* there is, somewhere, a physics teacher mumbling into a white board full of unintelligible symbols with his back to a class of bored teenagers.

Teacher attitudes and motivation are equally important. Here is an OFSTED inspector's view of one highly motivated teacher: "Clearly she felt that it was her responsibility to help all members of the class to learn and that if individuals experienced difficulties it was her 'failure'. I contrast this with the apparent ready willingness of some teachers to presume that difficulties that occur in their classes are a direct result of the limitations of the pupils."

There are many more teachers who are struggling with inadequate facilities, equipment, or even infrastructure. Perhaps more pertinently there are those whose main function is 'crowd control' rather than teaching. It only takes a few, or even one, disruptive member of a class to make a teacher's job difficult and to cause other potential learners to suffer.

> Just as we remember the inspiring teachers, most of us remember the poor teacher who 'put us off' a subject

Structural barriers ...

There is some evidence that class size affects the achievement (or otherwise) of young learners. This seems to be particularly true at pre-school and primary level and recent research into early brain development confirms this. Yet common sense suggests that it must also be relevant at secondary, further and higher levels of education (or why would Oxbridge guard so jealously their one-to-one tutorial systems?) and in vocational training also. The ultimate aim of the 'autonomous learner' may indeed be funding-led rather than learning-led.

Even at school level, subject *relevance* is considered a key factor. The Campaign for Learning's 1998 MORI survey found that 63% of children feel school 'does not prepare them for the real world'. This is in spite of the growth of GNVQs, the emphasis on key and core skills, education/ industry partnerships and a widening debate on learning to learn.

The question must therefore be asked as to whether more pertinent teaching might increase motivation in some learners.

At the further education level, whether or not a subject is perceived to be relevant to the learner is also a primary indicator of whether a student will succeed in, or even complete, a course. A FEDA research study[45] recently found that students are much more likely to 'drop out' if they feel they have been placed on an inappropriate course.

The same factors are equally true of adult training. In spite of the vast number of 'quality assurance' schemes that operate in the world of vocational training, getting onto a stimulating, useful, relevant course with a competent trainer can be a complete lottery. This is perhaps most true for those who are encouraged (or forced) onto training schemes. Here is a recipe...

Take one school leaver. Surround with images of people working, earning and buying. Add a large dollop of unemployment, a pint of boredom and several failed attempts to find work. Leave for a period of months or years. Remove any financial assistance. Interview, preferably using overworked and suspicious civil servant. Place on an inappropriate scheme some miles away. Add a poorly qualified or incompetent trainer, several other de-motivated trainees and place in bleak surroundings. Leave to simmer, stirring occasionally. Remove

from scheme and leave on shelf – possibly forever.
...for disaster.

Even where there is evidence that structured, relevant training has been provided, for example, in work-based training within large organisations, poor quality provision is not unknown. Far too few organisations measure the quality of the training that they make their workers and management undergo. Even fewer measure the efficacy of the training or its relevance and applicability in the workplace.

Short sighted

The commercial imperative means that in work-based training, far more than in formal education, delivery is led by the need to keep or improve profitability. Everything is (or should be) geared to the 'bottom line'.

However this can lead to a conflict between the needs or desires of the individual worker and those of the company.

Quite recently, Veronica McGivney wrote[46]: "There is abundant evidence that many employers do not believe they will reap the benefits from providing training since the workers concerned may use their enhanced skills to gain better jobs elsewhere; moreover, some may consider further investment in training unnecessary and not cost-effective, particularly if it conflicts with a policy to keep costs low through competitive tendering and increasing use of part-time and temporary, low-skilled labour. Firms competing for contracts will also want to keep their costs to a minimum, and training costs are not usually built into tenders."

Much more recently, a senior IT manager in a large company unwittingly referred to an institutional barrier to learning when he said: "Why should I provide training for my staff in software packages that will be of minimal benefit to us (the company) but will make them (the staff) much more valuable to others – including our rivals?"

This attitude, sometimes verging on the paranoid, seems to be prevalent throughout industry. Prue Leith has stated[47] that in the hotel business, the ones that train well (in spite of the fact that they have *much* better staff retention thus giving the lie to the 'losing good people' fear) are the exception.

Many employers do not believe they will reap the benefits from providing training

PAGE 53

Structural barriers ...

A company's training policy may reflect senior managers' own training/education or the lack of it

Add this fear (justified or not) to the current short-term perspectives of many businesses and a fairly large, employer-led, barrier begins to become apparent.

Several analyses have found that employee training in Britain is driven more by reaction to the immediate situation than by long-term aims[48].

This is perhaps a result of both the traumas and the opportunities that affected business during the 1980s. On the financial front this period was characterised by ever-changing stock and share movement and the short-term lending practice of banks and other financial institutions – businesses have thus tended to concentrate on profit targets and maximising investment returns. To some extent this attitude has continued throughout the 90s and certainly the pace of change has increased.

And while this ever increasing change has meant a concentration on the short term rather than longer-term issues such as training and R&D, it is also true that this pace has scared some companies out of training altogether. What is the point, ask some business owners, of training staff in skills that will be redundant almost as soon as they are learnt?

There may be a long-term training strategy but there are often contradictions between company training policy and actual practice. What top management say, and what line management and supervisors actually practice, are often worlds apart. Immediate circumstances, for example an urgent new order, can upset even seemingly set-in-stone training policy let alone ad hoc or 'needs must' policy, both of which are more prevalent in most organisations.

Some commentators suggest that a company's training policy may reflect senior managers' own training/education or the lack of it. In 1992, only 20% of senior managers in the UK were educated to degree level (compared with more than 60% in France and Germany and 85% in Japan and the US[49]). Some managers responsible for making decisions on employees' skill requirements are often themselves poorly educated and trained, especially older and more senior ones. The "I learned all I need to know in the University of Life" attitude is not yet dead.

Barriers to Learning

It seems there has been considerable movement, on this front at least, in the last few years. In 1990 only 10% of company directors prepared themselves for their role on the board. In 1998, 65% did so[50]. Many now undergo formal training for the role. This does suggest that a change of attitude is likely to 'trickle down' in the near future.

On the subject of employee qualifications, there is some evidence that many employers do not offer clear career routes to their employees nor value NVQs or the Accreditation of Prior Learning (APR). In their study of attitudes to training, eight years ago, Fuller and Saunders[51] wrote that there was: "A significant difference between employers' and employees' perceptions of the value of qualifications. While qualifications need to represent both 'use value' (accurately indicate an individual's competence) and 'exchange value' (have a wider currency to enable the holder to exchange qualifications for a better job or training), employers place more importance on use value and employees on exchange value."

Whilst this attitude might have been expected just four years after the launch of NVQs in 1986, a recent DfEE study[52] found that a majority of employers are still sceptical of their value. 'Too expensive', 'too time-consuming', 'lacking relevance and credibility', were some of the comments and the study concluded that the take-up of the qualifications across industrial sectors was unlikely to increase 'unless employers are persuaded of the commercial benefits the qualifications can bring'.

Long working hours are a further barrier to learning. Much training provision is available in the evening but an employee who is expected to stay late at work, who is still travelling home when the course starts, or who is simply too tired to attend is unlikely to partake of it. Fortunately there are now signs that the British 'long hours culture' is beginning to change. A new report[53] has found that: "Employers are now starting to recognise that persistent long hours result in diminishing returns to productivity and quality of work outputs, increased sickness absence, low morale and high staff turnover, and greater health and safety risks. Long hours also diminish family and social life and opportunities for community involvement. Employers presenting long hours as the expected norm

A majority of employers are still sceptical of NVQs

Structural barriers ...

may be unable to recruit those who take their outside responsibilities seriously."

A further problem is that while many companies, particularly SMEs, have severe skill shortages, they are unable to access training – even when they recognise the need. Partly this is a problem with bureaucratic and inflexible provision. For example, FE colleges, now major providers of vocational training, often offer courses at times and in places that suit them and the majority of their full-time students, but which do not at all suit the business providing the trainees. Modular courses and more emphasis on flexible and distance learning are gradually beginning to change this situation, but there is still a long way to go.

Special needs

A small proportion of the population face barriers to learning that none of the rest of us does, and ones that we often find hard to comprehend. Around 7% of those who responded to the *National Adult Learning Survey* in 1997 felt that their health problems or disability made learning difficult. The proportion of children who face this barrier is thought to be about the same. While the percentage may be relatively small, the actual number of people is in the order of four million.

There has, it should be said at the outset, been an enormous improvement in special needs recognition and learning provision over the last century. But there is still much that can and must be done, not least in changing the attitudes of the 'able-bodied' population.

There are two broad categories of 'disability' that need to be addressed here, physical factors and emotional ones. The physical sphere extends from serious motor disease and illnesses such as Down's Syndrome, to slight visual impairment or relatively minor hearing defects.

Neurological factors (for instance epilepsy or brain damage) will affect all areas of a child's or adult's learning. Whilst these need specialist medical and remedial help, it may be that a minor 'learning difficulty' can be a result of these and too many teachers and adult trainers are not sufficiently skilled to recognise the symptoms.

Barriers to Learning

Again, severe hearing or sight problems will be identified by medical tests, and will need special treatment, but minor ones are harder for an educator to spot, especially as, with children, these may be a temporary problem. Yet both can lead to a delay or even a long-term problem in reading and writing ability – factors which can cause a learning barrier that continues into and throughout adult life. There is much anecdotal evidence to suggest that a lack of recognition of a minor problem, by either an educator or medical specialist, can lead to major problems at a later date.

Poor manual or motor skills, which may be the result of illness, disability or merely result from immaturity, can also badly affect the ability to write and perform other manual tasks. The close link between reading and writing which is now recognised means that lack of progress in one is likely to lead to failure in the other.

At some stage everyone will suffer from an illness that will affect attendance at school, in further education or during adult education or training. However some are more prone to illness than others, particularly those from disadvantaged family backgrounds (of which more later). The effect on the continuity of learning, or the resulting impaired concentration, can result in long-term problems.

While physical illness (whether short-term or long) is more prevalent in children and older learners, emotional factors tend to affect all adults just as much. One in eight of the British population will suffer at some stage from depression or even psychotic illness. Work, relationships and family tensions can lead to emotional problems that can halt, interrupt or slow down the learning process at any age.

It is difficult to separate the structural barriers which can be created by an emotional upset or mental disorder from the personal ones that ensue – 'mental health' still being such a taboo subject outside certain specialist areas.

The luck of the draw

Social deprivation is, in the eyes of many if not most, commentators, the biggest of all the barriers to learning.

Alec Clegg[54] has itemised the differences and difficulties

> At some stage everyone will suffer from an illness that will affect their learning

Structural barriers ...

that disadvantaged children face and it is well worth reiterating this list here. In deprived or disadvantaged families:

- more children die young
- more children suffer ill health
- more have sick parents
- more live in areas where doctors are scarce
- more have parents who depend to some extent on their children's earnings
- more live in overcrowded homes
- more live in homes which lack the basic amenities
- more have parents who are school shy
- more have parents who left school as soon as they were able
- more are dependent on the social services
- more have come into contact with the probation service and with detention
- more live in an area where there is dirt and pollution
- more live in ugly derelict areas
- more attend old and ill-kept schools which are awaiting closure
- more come from homes where books are few
- more are taught by teachers who do not live in the area
- more are from impoverished families
- more are from families dependent on school meals
- more lack the facilities necessary to keep themselves clean
- fewer have parents who know their way about the education service
- fewer hear school English spoken in their homes
- fewer talk often with adults
- fewer read to their parents
- fewer have parents who read to them
- fewer have articulate parents
- fewer receive extra-curricular help
- fewer take enriching holidays
- fewer are taken to galleries or concerts by their parents
- fewer question their parents about school matters
- fewer have parents who could answer questions about school matters if asked
- fewer become prefects
- fewer are members of school teams
- fewer join youth clubs

Barriers to Learning

- fewer stay at school beyond the leaving age
- fewer experience success at school
- fewer take external examinations
- fewer succeed in those examinations when they take them
- fewer obtain jobs immediately on leaving school.

Research from the National Children's Bureau has shown us how potent these social impediments to learning can be. Clegg continues, "Children from large families are likely to be twelve months behind in their reading at the age of seven, children from homes with poor amenities eight months behind, children of parents who left school as soon as they legally could six months per parent behind, and the difference between the children of unskilled workers and those of the top professionals is a gap of seventeen months. It is curious that for so long we have failed to assess the full effect of environment, yet it is probably true to say that however stupid, no farmer on earth who had ten cows on scrub land and ten cows on good pasture would attribute the difference in milk yield to inheritance."

It is curious that for so long we have failed to assess the full effect of environment on learning

Structural barriers ...

- Finance:
    - Personal finance
    - Cost of courses
    - Tax /Benefit problems
    - Loss of income
    - Funding regimes
    - Changes in/withdrawal of
- Time constraints
- Lack of knowledge of learning opportunities
- Location/travel difficulties
- Childcare
- Disability provision
- Badly trained staff
- Too many qualifications
- Guidance/advice
- Jargon/acronyms
- Professional infighting
- Poor outreach provision
- Provider/learner conflicts
- Lack of relevance
- Parental pressures
- Disruptive classmates/fellow trainees
- Resources in schools/training centres
- Class sizes in schools (and FE)
- School streaming (and lack of)
- Subject selection (schools)
- Teacher/trainer numbers/ratio
- Lack of teacher/parent communication and school attitudes to parents
- Time, availability of courses etc
- Regional imbalances
- Poor feedback or measurement of progress
- Lack of management support in work-based learning
- Long working hours
- Competition between providers (and between guidance officers)

Barriers to Learning

A LACK of time and money are the most often quoted structural barriers to learning. The time barrier is cited most by two specific groups, those in work and those with caring responsibilities. Part-time and temporary workers often suffer most.

SMALLER businesses find particular problems with time for training. Some individuals feel they have alternative priorities for the use of leisure time – this relates back to a cultural barrier and forward to a personal one – motivation.

IN SPITE of an increase in education spending nationally, a lack of money to spend on learning is a common complaint from individuals. As well as the obvious costs of learning, such as course fees, there are many hidden costs and some 'below-the-line' ones. There are also many funding anomalies in our system. There are constant financial shifts in terms of the balance between state and individual and in terms of funding priorities.

TRAVEL difficulties and poor or non-existent child-care facilities present other barriers.

INADEQUATE guidance (the lack of good, impartial information on learning opportunities), the sheer range of courses, institutions and qualifications and poor provision for those with special needs are further structural barriers.

IN THE work place there is often a resistance from management to providing training and poor evaluation is all too common.

IN SCHOOLS, peer pressure, class sizes in schools and a lack of teacher/parent communication can present problems.

FINALLY, social deprivation is a major structural barrier.

CHAPTER 4

It is impossible to over estimate the importance of the family in providing and supporting learning

Personal barriers

Family values

IT IS possible to extract many of the more important structural barriers and discuss them in relation to the family – still our most important social unit. Structural and personal barriers overlap and merge when we consider the all-important issue of the attitude of an individual's family to learning.

Veronica McGivney reiterates one of the biggest barriers to learning[55]: "Certain sections of the community do not readily participate in education or training primarily because voluntary learning is perceived to be part of the culture pattern of higher socio-economic groups. Middle-class dominance in education is a difficult circle to break: members of higher socio-economic groups tend to live and work in environments where they have more scope for influencing their situation than those in lower income groups; where they have access to education or training opportunities; and where there is a positive orientation to education. They often come from families in which education was valued, have themselves been 'successful' in educational terms and have consequently passed on positive attitudes to education to their own children."

It is impossible to over estimate the importance of the family in providing learning and a positive (or otherwise) learning environment. Titus Alexander of Demos has written[56]: "Families are the foundation of education. Children spend less than 15% of their waking time in school between birth and school leaving age. Parents and other carers are responsible for 85% of a child's waking time. Many studies show that home background is the biggest influence on children's learning. Differences in support for learning at home are probably the greatest source of inequality in educational attainment among children of equal ability."

A great deal of learning happens in and around families – from birth onwards. Motor skills, learning language, personal development, communication, basic 'life' skills and taking on caring responsibilities, all are learned at home.

Parents do not get much support, financial or otherwise,

from the State, even though they are a child's first and most important learning provider. There are still very few parent education programmes available. Most help comes from other family members, friends or other informal networks and is often temporary and insufficient.

Where public spending is directed at families it tends to focus on child protection, assisting families under stress or dealing with the results of dysfunction. There is very little emphasis on prevention and even less on positive pro-active help.

Scientific studies[57] suggest that 50% of a child's intelligence and learning ability develops by the age of four, and 80% by the age of eight. The family situation is much more important than the school for translating these into measurable achievement. Differences between 'good' and 'bad' schools account for far less than features of the family or home. For example, there is a strong relationship between literary ability at the age of five and all later assessments of educational achievement.

Wendy Cooling of 'Bookstart' gives an example[58]: "Seven years ago I watched a group of rising fives on their first day at school. The teacher gave each child a picture book to look at, as she talked to parents reluctant to leave their children as they entered this challenging new phase in their lives. Most children looked at their books and turned the pages, one or two were obviously reading them, but one boy was lost – what was this thing he had been given? He sniffed it, tried to bend it, wondered if it was to be used like a Frisbee, or sat on; it seemed he had not met a book before. This child was starting school at a disadvantage, lacking the confidence and skills of his peers."

The family is all-important. Under the 'cultural' barriers to learning section in this report the importance of social class was considered. Children from professional and more financially stable backgrounds do better at school than other groups. More go on to FE or to university. But, says Titus Alexander[59], "Studies of successful young professionals from poor families show that enthusiastic parental involvement in their education is the common characteristic, *regardless* of social class."

There is one caveat to be put here. Alec Clegg provides a

50% of a child's intelligence and learning ability develops by the age of four, and 80% by the age of eight

Personal barriers ...

If the state could do more to help families, then so could schools

brief glimpse of the other side of the coin[60]: "It should not of course be thought that children born into affluence and comfort do not from time to time suffer. Indeed one of the worst fates that can befall a pupil of modest ability is to be the offspring of ambitious parents whose pressures are such that they are likely to give the child a loathing of the whole school learning process. And of course there are now many homes where children are given such lavish attention that they are insulated against the school's endeavours to stimulate, they become blasé, and what the teacher does to enliven learning is no more than tolerated."

The school and the family

If the state could do more to help families, then so could schools. Few schools involve parents sufficiently in their children's education. In many schools, particularly secondary ones, the communication between teachers and parents is poor or non-existent, simply involving a one way 'report' system and the occasional invitation to come in and 'discuss' (i.e. listen to) a child's progress. More work is needed on both formal and informal communication. Recognition by schools that parents are or should be the child's most important learning provider would go a long way to help.

Equally there is a need to turn back the trend for schools to act 'in loco parentis' at all times. As Elaine Applebee said in 1998[61], "The school curriculum is being put under pressure to compensate for the loss of some of the learning and socialisation which used to take place in the home or community. For example, the self-conscious focus on the transmission of morals, values and beliefs. Of course, schools and educational institutions have played their part in such transmission but now the expectation is that they have become key to that process."

She goes on to say that many of the issues which schools are being asked to address are not theirs to deal with alone and to discuss the inherent contradictions between what children are told at school and what they see at home: "Schools at the moment appear to be almost the last bastions of a community experience for many children and perhaps the

Barriers to Learning

Learning is not in itself a panacea for individuals' or society's problems

only place where adults, who are not related to them, take a keen interest in them. Persuading children and young people that education is the pathway out of poverty and social exclusion cannot just be the responsibility of schools, for the biggest influence on children is the reality of their parents' lives, and the lives of the community around them. If all they see are adults who have little control over their lives, ignored by decision-makers, abandoned by politicians, then the strong, positive messages which schools attempt to give to their children will be for nothing. So the work has to start in reconstructing our fractured communities and strengthening the families within them. Educators have a vested interest in this...and there are many examples of schools locally who endeavour to do what they can, often with no resources, to nurture burgeoning community activity."

The relationship between schools (and other learning environments) and the wider community is widely recognised, as is the fact that learning is not in itself a panacea for individuals' or society's problems. Veronica McGivney summarises this[62]: "A fundamental problem in working with deprived people is that education by itself cannot solve problems arising from social and economic factors, unemployment and racism. Adult educators recruiting new groups have to maintain a fine balance between giving

Personal barriers ...

Strength of motivation is a crucial factor which influences our level of achievement

people realistic expectations of what can be achieved through participation and not raising their hopes too high."

Can't or won't?

In the *National Adults Learning Survey*[63], all respondents (both learners and non-learners) were shown a number of cards each printed with a statement about a possible obstacle to taking part in learning activities. For each statement, respondents were asked to say whether or not it applied to them.

The most common obstacle to learning appeared to be a lack of interest – almost four in ten respondents (39%) said that they preferred to spend their free time doing things other than learning – men were more likely than women to state this preference (42% compared with 35%). A further 16% of the sample said that they were not interested in doing any learning, training or education; and a similar proportion (15%) said that they did not need to do any learning for the sort of work they wanted to do.

So over half of the total survey were uninterested in learning – lacking in any motivation to learn if you prefer. From the sheer numbers involved this would seem to be very worrying. Then add the fact that a lack of motivation is perhaps the biggest barrier of all, certainly the hardest to overcome, and the scale of this problem begins to emerge.

It is of course, not just adults who may be unmotivated or de-motivated. Ngaio Crequer has written[64]: "A child begins his or her life eager and curious to know the world, reaching out and touching what is not yet understood. Sometimes it comes apart in their hands. The light (this light of curiosity) goes out as they make the inexorable march into the formal education system."

Peter Mortimore[65], links lack of motivation to under-achievement in schools: "Strength of motivation is a crucial factor which influences our level of achievement. The de-motivating effects of 'failure' at the critical points of education (11, 15/16, and 18) are well documented."

So which came first, the lack of motivation or the under-achievement? The two are inextricably linked, as are many other issues.

Barriers to Learning

The reasons for dislike of or non-participation in learning are a complex and interacting mix of external and internal factors. Lack of time and finance are the most frequently *cited* barriers to adult participation in post-compulsory education and training. Children are more likely to be straightforward and say 'school is boring,' or 'I can't see the point' (for example 34% of 11-16 year olds say they have problems with their school work because they are bored[66]). But, for both children and adults, it is becoming more and more apparent that cultural, attitudinal, dispositional or psychological factors play a crucial role.

Wanting to learn after school has ended seems to depend on a young person's 'learning identity' – that is how people conceive of themselves as learners (or not). Lifelong learning – as an attitude or an aptitude – ought to begin during years spent at school, but for significant numbers of young people school turns off the learning impulse, possibly for good. Their experiences during compulsory education convince the 'worst' cases not only that they have nothing to learn but that they can never be enthusiastic learners. In the NALS survey, men were more likely then women to say that they had not enjoyed learning at school (19% compared with 15%).

Veronica McGivney[67] writes, "It is well established that many people who left school at an early age without qualifications associate education with 'boredom, irrelevance and failure'. Subsequent work experience may provide little evidence that further education or training will be of value to them. In their survey of attitudes to training, Fuller and Saunders[68] found that unskilled workers did not see any connection between formal training and jobs such as labouring and cleaning, while semi-skilled workers did not see how it would help them improve their performance or gain promotion. The researchers conclude that one of the most important disincentives to train may be the 'uneven connection between training, qualifications and career progression'."

Cultural barriers (for example racism or ageism) may cause de-motivation. Structural barriers (lack of money, poor provision) may compound it. But one of the central questions is: Is a lack of motivation caused wholly or mainly

> **Compulsory education convinces some not only that they have nothing to learn but that they can never be enthusiastic learners**

Personal barriers ...

by external factors? Or is there, in some people, an *intrinsic* dislike of or detachment from learning? These are complex issues.

In the last century most educators would have considered that certain sectors of society, and nearly all the individuals within them, were either incapable of learning or only able to learn at a very basic level. The notion of the 'incapable learner' was as widespread as that of the 'undeserving poor'.

Today, while the second concept is almost completely defunct, the first lingers on and leads to the labelling of people, adults as well as children, as thick, slow or stupid.

Lack of self-confidence and self-esteem are prime causes (and effects) of these attitudes. Lack of motivation can easily become a vicious circle, with those who feel they 'can't' do something facing a much greater barrier than those who simply won't. And there is no doubt that this lack is prevalent in most groups of non-learners and under-achievers.

Certain groups are more likely to suffer from low self-esteem (and therefore more likely to be unmotivated) than others. Some groups of women seem particularly affected. A European Conference on educational research found that, "Although women invest more than men in education, the school-to-work transition result does not improve – this can lead to a lack of self esteem and a 'what's the point?' attitude."

Women are more likely than men to be worried about their lack of ability. In the NALS survey, 17% said that they did not have the necessary qualifications for most courses, and a similar proportion (17%) said that they would be worried about keeping up with other people on the course.

Lack of self-confidence may manifest itself in shyness or reserve – true of both adults and quiet children: "Classroom observations reveal that class or group discussions are often dominated by a small number of confident, not necessarily articulate children. Many other children remain silent, frequently showing reluctance to join in the social and academic discourse. The fact that quiet, seemingly compliant, behaviour does not pose an obvious threat to classroom discipline means that the educational and emotional needs of quiet pupils often go undetected." Some of the emotional, psychological, practical and social factors that inhibit pupils

thus form barriers to communication, learning and self-esteem.

Recognising that motivation was the key to learner participation, Crowder and Pupyin[69], found that: "It is an individual's *expectations* of a learning exercise that will determine whether they are sufficiently motivated to pursue it. As long as their perception of learning and its outcomes remains unchanged, their expectation of it will remain unchanged and it will not be possible to entice people back into learning without first altering their perception of the value of that learning to them personally."

The concept of the vicious circle is well-explained by the same two authors: "While non-learners can be encouraged/pressured to undertake learning activities, they cannot be forced to perceive the learning positively. Non-learners who are involuntarily involved in learning may remain convinced that learning will not benefit them. They are therefore unlikely to put in much effort and, as a result, are less likely to achieve positive outcomes. This in turn will confirm the individual's view that learning is not useful for them."

Without motivation there can be no real learning. But motivation can come from different sources. Christopher Ball has asked[70], "Is a 'learning society' individualistic – can individuals be relied upon to seek out learning opportunities and acquire skills? We learn if the boss insists on it, or learn in order to get a credential. But in a 'learning society' don't we one way or another have to internalise an idea of ourselves as learning for the love of it or, as seems still to be the case in Germany, because the culture demands it?"

The old story

If much of this chapter on personal barriers to learning has rightly concentrated on the problems of a lack of motivation caused at an early age (sometimes very early) and reinforced in the formal education system, the results can be seen right through an individual's life. A significant group in the NALS survey (13% of the sample) said that they were 'too old to learn'.

Most available research shows a fall-off in learning at retirement age, particularly among men. Partly of course

It will not be possible to entice people back into learning without first altering their perception of the value of that learning

Personal barriers ...

Continued learning benefits older people physically and mentally

this is the effect of leaving work and, with it, the opportunities for continuous professional development and vocational training. Sometimes it is the result of there being no further incentive to undertake any formal learning now that 'work' is over. But most often it seems simply that the attitude is that learning is for young (or younger) people.

The flip-side to this is the amount of informal or 'leisure' learning that older people undertake. Much of this goes unrecognised as Stephen Gorrard notes[71]: "If leisure learning is a characteristic of later life learners, surely it is a characteristic that creators of a learning society seek to enhance? But this self-reliance may be negated by 'the audit society'. The hobbyists are informal learners, learning at home in their spare time, not seeking certification and not linking learning to their work and they may be disappearing in association with the growth in formal participation. There is a tradition of 'autodidacts' and hobbyists outside work who are not yet included in the supposedly 'inclusive' learning society of today. Do they have to certify their activities, or pay a provider to gain recognition?"

Physical or mental disabilities, ill-health and other factors which are a mixture of structural and personal barriers (and are covered in the previous chapter) are all more likely to affect older learners and non-learners than their younger peers. There is no doubt that, as a person gets older, there is a physical deterioration (in the body as well as the brain) which can affect the ability and the motivation to learn. Significantly, recent research has also shown that continued learning appears to help people maintain their physical and mental acuity.

A sense of style

Much has been written on different learning styles and can be easily accessed elsewhere. But it should be mentioned here that a major barrier to learning can be the imposition of an inappropriate style of learning or learning technique on an individual or group. In Honey and Mumford's four categories of learning types (active, reflective, pragmatic, theoretical) forcing one type to undertake learning in an

unsuitable way or context is like trying to bash the proverbial square peg into a round hole. Resistance and even damage may result.

In the 1998 Campaign for Learning MORI poll, respondents were asked to list their preferred way(s) of learning. 45% preferred learning on their own through self-study, 33% would rather be with a group and under instruction.

Far too few schools, and other learning centres, recognise the importance of discovering how individuals learn when, in reality, respect for the learner should be paramount.

There is, says head teacher Kevin Satchwell, no secret recipe[72]: "Running successful schools is not complicated. Educating children is not rocket science, but we tend to make schools into complex organisations and then look for complex explanations when we don't succeed. All that it takes is to know how you teach effectively and how you help children to learn effectively. Effective teaching involves knowing your children as people, and knowing where they are in their learning."

The same sentiments could be applied to almost all areas of adult learning.

Brain waves

How a person learns is the latest and one of the most significant developments in understanding some of the personal barriers to learning. And one of the more interesting scientific/learning developments of the last few years has been an increased understanding of how the brain actually works.

Until the latter part of this century, little was known at a scientific or technical level about the structure and operation of the brain. Educators thus assumed that it was 'an empty vessel waiting to be filled'. Children were born with a few innate characteristics but beyond that were blank slates. And their very early experiences were seen to be of little significance; learning began at school.

In the late 1960s the metaphor shifted to that of a linear computer waiting to be programmed, and so external inputs, not motivation, were seen to drive learning.

But, as John Abbott explained recently[73], "Brain research

> **Far too few learning centres recognise the importance of discovering how individuals learn when, in reality, respect for the learner should be paramount**

Personal barriers ...

We are driven as much by emotion as by logic

now describes 'predispositions' inherited from our evolutionary past which are best described as a collection of 'successful adaptation skills'. Critical to the brain's healthy development are prenatal health, a challenging, stimulating and reassuring environment in the first four or five years of life followed by plenty of opportunity to develop practical involvement in the growth years, and personal responsibility during adolescence.

"Stimulation, in a low threat environment, causes the brain to function, process and 'learn' more effectively. Too much stimulation, however, at any stage in life, turns a challenge into a threat. The brain deals with this easily. It just 'downshifts' or literally turns off. To effectively work at challenging tasks, research is now suggesting, requires significant amounts of reflective time. Learning is very much a reflective activity. 'I need to go away and think that over' is a critical part of brain functioning. It is not a practical strategy to apply in a normal classroom!

"All this is done spontaneously in response to challenge. The brain does not have to be taught to learn. Learning is what it does – automatically. To thrive it needs plenty of stimulation, and it needs suitable feedback systems. Effective learning is dependent upon emotional energy. We are driven (the ancestral urges of long ago) as much by emotion as by logic. Children who learn because they simply want to work something out because it matters to them, are far more resilient and determined when they face problems than children who seek external rewards. The same goes for adults. Intrinsic motivation is far more significant than extrinsic. When in trouble the first group searches for novel solutions, while the latter looks for external causes to blame for their failure. The brain is essentially a survival system; it takes seriously those things which matter to it. Emotional well-being may well be more essential – to the brain – for survival than intellectual.

"Since no two brains are alike, no enriched environment will completely satisfy any two individuals for an extended period of time. No matter what form the enrichment takes, it is the challenge that matters; passive observation is not enough, it is interactivity that is so essential. 'Tell me and I

Barriers to Learning

forget. Show me and I remember. Let me do and I understand,' says the ancient Chinese proverb."

The brain learns best, and learns to grow more, when it is exercised in highly challenging but low-threat environments. Learning and emotion cannot be separated.

Both John Abbott, in the work of the 21st Century Learning Initiative, and others such as Geoffrey Caine, strongly propose that any new methods of learning must take what is beginning to be known of how the brain works crucially into account. Caine contends that there is an optimum state of mind for learning and that the individual (or others) can create this[74].

"The basic beliefs about learning held by many is far too limited, and problems cannot be solved until these beliefs are changed – but there is a coherent way to look at the problems. With the advent of a new view of life and the universe given to us by biology and physics, along with the prolific use of technology, and a new understanding of ourselves, we are leaving behind a way of looking at the world that is built on a belief in stability and controlled change as ideal. What is emerging is an understanding of the dynamism of life at every level."

New research into the functioning of the brain offers radical ways of understanding how we learn and behave as individuals and in groups. Thus one of the major personal barriers to learning is that none of our structures, whether schools colleges or businesses, nor most of our attitudes, yet take sufficient account of this.

As John Abbott says, "The most significant barrier to learning is our lack of resolution to use the information that we have to carry out a radical transformation of systems of learning which simply do not go with the grain of the brain."

Once again a personal barrier becomes one that is, at first sight, structural, but has a deeper underlying cultural significance.

Any new methods of learning must take what is known of how the brain works into account

Personal barriers ...

Barriers to Learning

CERTAIN sections of the community do not readily participate in education or training primarily because voluntary learning is seen as for other (maybe richer) groups. Family pressures can determine learning participation or the lack of it.

INDIVIDUAL motivation is a crucial factor. This can be influenced by many factors including peer pressure, social pressures, and lack of support from teachers.

INDIVIDUALS will not learn if there is no perceived reward – however this reward may be measured.

NON-LEARNERS can get caught in a vicious circle of low expectations.

RESPECT for the learner is not sufficiently widespread nor is the recognition that people, including children, all have different learning styles.

THERE is far too little recognition of how we learn. Our brains cope with learning best in highly challenging but low-threat environments. None of our structures, nor most of our attitudes, yet take account of this.

CONCLUSION

If we want to change the nature of our society and create an appetite for learning then action is needed on all three fronts simultaneously

The chicken and the egg

AS WAS stated at the outset, barriers to learning do not always dovetail neatly into the three categories described.

Apart from the technology example given in Chapter One, there are others which cross the boundaries: unemployment is a cultural barrier and needs political and social change to provide a lasting solution. Yet it is also an important structural barrier and embraces other structural ones – finance, guidance and accessibility for example.

If we truly want to change the nature of our society and create an appetite for learning that will lead, over time, to the development of a true lifetime learning culture, then action is needed on all three fronts simultaneously.

On the cultural front, effort is necessary for us to move towards economic and societal justice, not just through increased education. There needs, perhaps, to be a recognition that learning is not only useful when it is narrow and job-related. More recognition of the importance of informal learning and its value to individuals and society would be a good start. As Stephen Gorrard puts it[75]: "Greater inclusion in a learning society may come more easily from greater recognition of tacit knowledge rather than more participation."

Recognising or identifying the barriers to learning which exist is the first step on the thousand-mile journey to overcoming them. It is easy to recognise some barriers; they leap out at you. Here is one brief case study:

WISE (Women into Science and Engineering) received a request for help from a potential student. The enquirer was a mature student (38), a woman and a single parent. Because of her previous experience, she had been accepted straight into the second year of a B.Eng. degree course in geological engineering.

She was exactly the sort of learner that the current rhetoric around lifetime learning is meant to encourage, yet she had been thwarted in her attempts to find funding. All she was guaranteed was a small mandatory grant (about £800) from her local authority and the opportunity to take out a loan of about £2,000. Her travel, maintenance and child-care needs

meant she required about £5,000 – £6,000 a year. Not much by engineering salary standards but a brick wall to her.

Sadly, WISE were unable to help, nor could any of the engineering institutes or other bodies. The Government was not interested. The University staff were sympathetic but could offer little else. Instead of heading towards a degree and probably a job in an occupation where professionals, and especially women, are in short supply, she is now working part-time in an unrelated field.

Sometimes the brick wall is barely visible. David Ashton wrote, in 1998[76]: "In one company, employees face many barriers in their efforts to learn, not because the company deliberately erected them, indeed the company were unaware of them, but because the process of learning is contentious. The parties involved had different agendas and in many cases were not aware of how to facilitate the process (of learning)."

The nature of the subject matter of this guide has meant that a somewhat negative tone prevails throughout. But it is not all doom and gloom. Much is being done to diminish many of the barriers to learning; particularly the structural ones, and examples of good practice will form the basis of this guide's companion volume, *Overcoming Barriers to Learning*.

It has become clear that cultural barriers are the most difficult to deal with, that structural barriers are the most numerous but that personal barriers, particularly those involving motivation and learning styles, are the most important.

Overcome the motivational barrier and the others, however large, seem less daunting and more manageable. Not all barriers can be easily overcome but increasing motivation is the most necessary first step on the proverbial thousand-mile journey. Create an appetite for learning, at each and every level, and everything else will gradually follow.

Examples of good practice will form the basis of a companion volume, *Overcoming Barriers to Learning*

TEXT REFERENCES

1 The Learning Age, a renaissance for a New Britain, DfEE Green Paper, 1998
2 Attitudes to Learning MORI State of the Nation Survey, Ed Greany, T. CfL, 1998
3 National Adult Learning Survey, DfEE, 1998
4 Sargant, N. et al, The Learning Divide, NIACE/Gallup, 1997
5 See CfL MORI poll for full definition
6 ibid
7 Ashton, D. Skill Formation: Redirecting the Research Agenda in Learning at Work, Coffield, F. Ed, 1997
8 National Adult Learning Survey, DfEE, 1998
9 Fryer, R. Learning for the 21st Century, ESRC, 1998
10 McGuire, M. Working to Learn, People Management, IPD, 1997
11 Lucas, B. Creating the Learning Age, article in 't' magazine, June 1998
12 Ainscow, M, Reaching Out to All Learners: Opportunities and Possibilities, Presentation at the North of England Education Conference, 1998
13 Tuckett, A. Barriers to Participation in Learning, from 'For Life', CfL 1996
14 Women's Attitudes to Learning, CfL, 1998
15 Lindley, R. Women's Employment, EOC/HMSO, 1992
16 Sanderson, K. and Turner, J. Women's Training, An Evaluation of Current Provision; Women's Employment, Enterprise and Training Unit. 1992
17 MORI survey for the Older and Bolder initiative, NIACE 1995
18 Schuler, T. Carnegie Third Age Enquiry, 1991
19 Bayliss, V. Redefining Work. 1998
20 OECD, Report into Lifelong Learning, 1996
21 Letter in Education Guardian, Sept 1998
22 Kennedy, H. Widening Participation in Further Education, FEFC, 1996
23 Speaking at CfL colloquium on 'Turning Learning Theory into Practice, 1996
24 Bayliss, B. in Redefining Work, RSA 1998
25 De kwalitatieve structuur van de werkgelegenheid in Nederland, OSA 1997
26 Applebee, E. Speech to the North of England Education Conference, 1998
27 Ball, C. in For Life, RSA/CfL, 1995
28 Toynbee, P. Equipped for Life, from Challenges Facing Future Britain, ESRC, 1998
29 Coffield, F. Why's the beer always stronger up North?, ESRC, 1998
30 Linton, J. Keeping Talent Switched On, Training Tomorrow, Jan 1997
31 Sargant, N. Learning & Leisure, NIACE, 1991
32 Research study by NIACE, 1994
33 Women's Attitudes to Learning, CfL, 1998
34 *Push* guide to Which University, 1999
35 Speaking Up, Speaking Out, Industrial Society 1997
36 Women's Attitudes to Learning, CfL, 1998
37 Evans, D. writing in 't' magazine, 1998
38 Fryer, R. Learning for the 21st Century, DfEE, 1998
39 9,000 Voices, FEDA research report into student drop-out rates and reasons, 1998
40 The Childcare Gap, Report by the Daycare Trust 1997
41 Spurling, A. Guidance Matters, 't' magazine, June 1997
42 Survey by S. Ball of King's College, quoted in Challenges Facing Future Britain, ESRC, 1998
43 Pardey, D. Building Bridges Further, NEBS Management, 1998

44 Fryer, R. Learning for the 21st Century, DfEE, 1998

45 9,000 Voices, FEDA research report into student drop-out rates and reasons, 1998

46 McGivney, V. Wasted Potential, NIACE, 1994

47 Speech to the Training for Tomorrow conference, 1993

48 (DfEE, Small Businesses and Training Needs, Skills and Enterprise Briefing No. 20 1992)

49 Finegold, D. National Commission on Education Briefing 1992

50 Sign of the Times, Institute of Directors report, 1998

51 [51] Fuller, A. & Saunders, M. Potential Take-up of Mass Training, Lancaster University, 1990

52 NFER report into take-up of N/SVQs, DfEE, 1998

53 Kodz, J. Long Hours Culture, IES Research report, 1999

54 Clegg, A. Acknowledging Disadvantages, from 'Teaching and Learning in Secondary Schools' 1997

55 McGivney, V. Education's for Other People, 1991

56 Alexander, T. Family Learning, Demos, 1997

57 Bloom, B.S. Stability & Change in Human Characteristics, Wiley, 1964

58 Cooling, W. Quoted in the TES, Sept 1998

59 Alexander, T. Family Learning, Demos, 1997

60 Clegg, A. Acknowledging Disadvantages, from 'Teaching and Learning in Secondary Schools' 1997

61 Applebee, E. Speech to the North of England Education Conference, 1998

62 McGivney, V. Education's for Other People, 1991

63 National Adult Learning Survey, DfEE, 1998

64 Crequer, N. From the FE section in For Life, Campaign for Learning, 1995

65 Mortimore, P. Tackling Underachievement – A Guide to Successful Practice, 1998

66 From: Speaking Up, Speaking Out! 20/20 Vision survey by the Industrial Society 1997

67 McGivney, V. Motivating Unemployed Adults, NIACE 1992

68 Fuller, A. & Saunders, M. Potential Take-up of Mass Training, Lancaster University, 1990

69 Crowdeer, N. Pupynin K, Understanding Learner Motivation, DfEE, 1995

70 Interview In Training Tomorrow magazine, 1995

71 Gorard, S. et al, Participation in adult education and training in an industrial area, Cardiff University 1997

72 Quoted in the Times Educational Supplement, Sept 1998

73 Abbott, J. Reported in the Parliamentary Monitor, Sept. 1998

74 Caine, R. & G. Education on the Edge of Possibility, 1997

75 Gorard, S. et al, Participation in adult education and training in an industrial area, Cardiff University 1997

76 Ashton, D. Skill Formation, quoted in Learning at Work, 1998

SELECT BIBLIOGRAPHY and further reading

9,000 Voices, FEDA research report into student drop-out rates and reasons, 1998

A

Abbot, J. More than just schooling, The Journal, 21st Century Learning Initiative, 1998

Addams, B. Listening To You, Listening To Us: Expanding education provision for unemployed adults in Birmingham. FEU/REPLAN. 1987

Adlington, E. Educational Vouchers for Unemployed Adults. NIACE/REPLAN. 1988

Ainscow, M. Reaching Out to All Learners: Opportunities and Possibilities, Presentation at the North of England Education Conference, 1998

Akins, A. Barriers to access to learning opportunities in New Zealand. ACE Bulletin 15, pp25-28. 1985

Allen, G. Community Education: An agenda for educational reform. Open University Press. 1988

Alloway, J. & Nelson, P. Advice and Guidance to Individuals. SIACE/UDACE. 1987

Ames, J. Financial Barriers to Access. UDACE. 1986

Analoui, F. Training and Transfer of Learning, Avebury, 1993

Applebee, E. Speech to the North of England Education Conference, 1998

Argyris, C. 'Teaching Smart People How to Learn' Harvard Business Review Vol 9, 1991

Ashton, D. Skill Formation: Redirecting the Research Agenda in Learning at Work, Coffield, F. Ed, 1997

Attitudes to Learning MORI State of the Nation Survey, CfL, 1998

B

Barr, J. Keeping a low profile: adult education in Scotland. Adult Education, 59,4. 1987

Bartolome, F. 'Nobody Trusts the Boss Completely, Now What', Harvard Business Review Vol 67, 1989

Barwuah, A. & Andrews, M. Widening participation on inner city estates, FEDA, 1999

Bateson,G. Radical community education in local authority settings – a contradiction in terms? Journal of Community Education, 6, 4, pp21-23. 1988

Bayliss, V, Redefining Work, RSA, 1998

Beder, H. & Valentine, T. Iowa's Basic Education Students: Descriptive profiles based on motivation, cognitive ability and socio-demographic variables. Department of Education, Iowa. 1987.

Bentley, T. Learning Beyond the Classroom,

Bird, M. & Varlaam, A. Changing Course: Community education in Inner London. Reports PS 7114, ILEA. 1987

Blamire, J. & Neilsen, F. Don't Call Us. REPLAN. 1987

Bloomer, M. & Hodkinson, P. Moving into FE, FEDA, 1997

Bourner, T. & Hamed, M. Non-standard Entry Students: Entry qualifications and degree performance. CNAA Development Services Publication 10. CNAA. 1987

Bourner, T. et.al. Students on CNAA's Part-time first Degree Courses. CNAA Development Service Publication 16. CNAA. 1988

Bridger, S. Women Learning: A consumer view of access provision. Bradford Women's Employment Group. 1987

Brown, J. Some aspects of access to adult education. Journal of Community Education, 6, 2. 1987

C

Caine, R. & G. Education on the Edge of Possibility, 1997

Calder, J. (ed). Disaffection and Diversity: Overcoming the barriers for adult learners, The Falmer Press. 1992

Cannon, P. Thoughts on adult education. AONTAS Newsletter, 1, 9, p6. 1988

Careers Service, Moving On, 1996

Careers Service, Survey of disaffected young people, 1996

Castle, E. & Selby, A. Then and now: a course for old people. Adult Education, 60, 2, pp122-126.1987

Centre for Labour Market Studies. Training in the Recession, University of Leicester. 1993

Challis, J. Building and Communication: Report on MSC-sponsored linked-skills project at the Lee Centre 1981-82

Charnley, A.H. Fees Charged to Part-time Students in LEAs 1988-98. NIACE. 1989

Chatfield, M. & Mills, J. The Bridge Project: training for women in Washington. Working with Women Bulletin 1. REPLAN. 1987

Clegg, A. Acknowledging Disadvantages, from 'Teaching and Learning in Secondary Schools' 1997

Clifford, P. Unemployed Men and Adult Education in Milton Keynes. Milton Keynes Community Education. 1986

Coffield, F. A National Strategy for Lifelong Learning, University of Newcastle, 1996

Coffield, F. Why's the beer always stronger up North? ESRC, 1998

Cole, P. Dearne Valley Project, Annual Report 1985-86. Northern College. 1986

Colwell, D. Factory Project Report. ALFA: Access to Learning for Adults. The North London Open College Network. 1988

Cookson, P.S. The nature of the knowledge base of adult education: the example of participation. Educational Considerations V, XIV. 1987

Cooling, W. Quoted in the TES, Sept 1998

Cooper, M. & Bornat, J. Equal opportunity or special need: combating the woolly bunny. An assessment of the work of the ILEA Education Resource Unit for Older People. Journal of Education Gerontology, 3, 1. 1988

Crowdeer, N. Pupynin, K. Understanding Learner Motivation, DfEE, 1995

D

Darkenwald, G. G. Comparison of Deterrents to Adult education Participation in Britain and the United States. SCUTREA. 1988

Darkenwald, G.G. & Valentine, T. Factor structure of deterrents to public participation in adult education. Adult Education Quarterly, 35, 4, pp177-193. 1985

Darkenwald, G.G. & Hayes, E. Assessment of adult attitudes towards continuing education. International Journal of Lifelong Education. 1987

Davies, P. What makes for a satisfied student, FEDA, 1999

De kwalitatieve structuur van de werkgelegenheid in Nederland, OSA 1997

DeBell, D. & Davies, B. Paying for Skills: Financial barriers to access to vocational training for adults, City College, Norwich. 1991

Demos Collection, Family Learning, 1997

Demos Collection, Relative Values, 1997

Demos Collection, The Wealth and Poverty of Networks, 1997

DfEE, Employers' Attitudes To Individual commitment to learning, 1993

DfEE, Extending Opportunity, National framework for study support, 1998

DfEE, Further Education for the New Millennium, 1998

DfEE, Lifetime Learning: A consultation document, 1996

DfEE, Maximising Potential, New options for learning after 16, 1996

DfEE, Small Businesses and Training Needs, Skills and Enterprise Briefing No. 20 1992

DfEE, Turning Research into Action – Providers' attitudes to learning, 1996

DfEE, Understanding Learner Motivation, 1994

Select bibliography and further reading ...

Duke, F. Degrees of experience: are the needs and expectations of mature adults and school-leavers compatible? Journal of Access Studies, Spring 1,1, pp54-63. 1987

E

Economic and Social Research Council, Challenges Facing Future Britain, 1998

Edwards, J. Working-class Education in Liverpool: a radical approach. University of Manchester. 1986

Eldred, E.J. An exploration of the experiences of non-participant long-term unemployed and their attitudes towards continuing education. Unpublished dissertation, University of Sheffield. 1987

Elliot, Larry, The Education Ethos, The Guardian, Oct 1997

Employment Service, Defining employability, 1997

Evans, N. The Assessment of Prior Experiential Learning. CNAA Development Service Publication 17. CNAA. 1988

F

Falken, G. A black model of community education. Journal of Community Education, 6, 4, pp4-6. 1988

Finch, J. & Rustin, M. a Degree of Choice? Higher education and the right to learn. Penguin Books. 1986

Finegold, D. National Commission on Education Briefing 1992

Finegold, D. Breaking Out of the Low-skill Equilibrium, National Commission on Education Briefing no. 5. 1992

Fraser, A. Access to Employment in Childcare and Nursery Education for Bengali Women. Tower Hamlets AEI. 1988

Fraser, L. & Ward, K. Education from

Everyday Living: An assessment of community-based courses with unemployed people. NIACE/REPLAN. 1988

Fryer, R. Learning for the 21st Century, DfEE, 1998

Fuller, A. & Saunders, M. Potential Take-up of Mass Training, Lancaster University, 1990

Fulton, O. & Ellwood, S. Admissions to Higher Education: Policy and practice. Training Agency. 1989

G

Geraint-Evans, J. Adult Basic Education in Powys, 1983-85. ALBSU Development Project Final Report. ALBSU. 1986

Gerry, J. Director Development, in 't' magazine, July 1998

Gooderham, P.N. Reference group theory and adult education. Adult Education Quarterly, 37, 3, pp140-151. 1987

Gorard, S. et al, Participation in adult education and training in an industrial area, Cardiff University 1997

Gorard, S. Furlong, J. Fevre, R. Rees, G. How to spot a lifelong learner at 40 paces! Cardiff University

Gorard, S. Furlong, J. Fevre, R. Rees, G. The Learning Society, Cardiff University

Gray, E. First Year Report of the Open University Community Education Project, Feb 1986-Feb 1987. Open University National Community Programme Agency. 1988

H

Hills, A. Link Into Learning: Report on the ALBSU special development project in Richmond Adult and Community College, July 1984-March 1986. ALBSU. 1987

Holmes, J. & Storrie, T. Consett – A Case

Study of Education and Unemployment. FEU. 1985

Holtzclaw, L.R. Flexible admission practices for adult learners. Lifelong Learning, April, pp9-11. AAACE. 1988

I

Industrial Society, Self Managed Learning, 1997

Industrial Society, Speaking Up, Speaking Out, 1997

IPD, Working to Learn – A Partnership Approach, 1998

Issitt, M. & Spence, J. An exploration of the relationship between community education and higher education. Journal of Community Education, 6, 4a, pp14-17. 1988

Issitt, M. Organising women's health days, Journal of Community Education, 6, 1988

J

James, R. Defining Employability: report from an open workshop. 1998

Johnstone, D. Further Opportunities, Cassell.1995

Johnstone, R. Exploring the Educational Needs of Unwaged Adults. NIACE/REPLAN. 1987

Jones, B. Educating Ritas. Times Higher Education Supplement. 1988

Jones, D. Access to the Arts: Adult education and cultural development. Routledge. 1988

K

Kearney, P. Second Chance to Learn: Final report. WEA Berks, Bucks and Oxon. 1987

Kennedy, H. Widening Participation in Further Education, FEFC, 1996

Kettley, P. Strebler M, *Changing Roles for Senior Managers*, IES Report no 327, 1997

Kitchen, P. Give us more of the cake. Journal of Community Education, 6, 4, pp19-21. 1988

Kodz, J. Long Hours Culture, IES Research report, 1999.

L

Lambers, K. Women Returners in Education: Conference report. Polytechnic of the South Bank/Open College of South London. 1988

Lawson, A. Older unemployed Adults Project. Liverpool City College/REPLAN. 1988

Lewis, L. An issue of support. International Journal of Lifelong Education, 4, 2, pp163-176. 1988

Liddington, J. What do you do after a 'New Opportunities' course? Adult Education, 61, 1, pp36-40. 1988

Lindley, R. Women's Employment, EOC/HMSO, 1992

Linton, J. Keeping Talent Switched On, Training Tomorrow, Jan 1997

Literacy Task Force, The Implementation of the National Literacy Strategy, 1997

Longworth, N. & Davies, K. Lifelong Learning – New Vision

Lowen, D. Barriers to Educational Opportunities for Adults. A report on the institutional barriers to educational opportunities for adults. Central and West London Open College. 1986

Lucas, B. Creating the Learning Age, article in 't' magazine, June 1998

M

Macadam, M. & Sutcliffe, J. Still a Chance to Learn? NIACE, 1996

Mace, J. A Time and a Place: A study of education and manual work,1983-84. Lee

Select bibliography and further reading ...

Centre, Goldsmiths' College. 1985

Mace, J. & Yarnit, M. (eds). Time Off To Learn: Paid educational leave and low-paid workers. Methuen. 1987

Macfarlane, R. Unshackling the Poor, Rowntree Foundation, 1997

Maloney, K. Priming the system, REPLAN Review 4, DES/REPLAN, 1989

McGivney, V. Education's for Other People, NIACE, 1991

McGivney, V. Motivating Unemployed Adults, NIACE 1992

McGivney, V. Staying or Leaving the course? NIACE, 1996

McGivney, V. Wasted Potential, NIACE, 1994

McIlroy, J. & Spencer, B. University Adult Education in Crisis. University of Leeds. 1988

McPherson, J. Development of Co-ordinated Adult Education and Training Provision in a Rural Area. FEU. 1986

Mellander, K. The Power of Learning, ASTD, 1996

Metcalf, H. Class and Higher Education, CIHE, 1997

Mills, J. Funding for women's courses. Working with Women Bulletin 2. REPLAN. 1988

Mills, J. The Bridge Project: Training for women in Washington. Washington Tyne and Wear Bridge Project. 1986

MORI survey for the Older and Bolder initiative, NIACE 1995

Mortimore, P. Tackling Underachievement – A Guide to Successful Practice, 199

Moss, W. Breaking the Barriers. ALFA/REPLAN. 1987

Munn, P. & MacDonald, C. Adult Participation in Education and Training. SCRE. 1988

N

NACETT, Skills for 2000, 1997

National Adult Learning Survey, DfEE, 1998

Neville, C. Education and Change: A survey of users of an education advice service. 1986

New Start, Facing the Challenge, November 1997

NFER, report into take-up of N/SVQs, DfEE, 1998

Nicholl, N. Older Adults. REPLAN Project report. Sandown College/REPLAN. 1988

Norris, C. Towards a theory of participation in adult education. Adult Education, 58, 2, pp120-122. 1985

Norwich College, Paying for skills: Financial barriers to training

O

OECD, Lifelong Learning for All, 1997

P

Pardey, D. Building Bridges Further, NEBS Management, 1998

Parliamentary Monitor, Sept. 1998

Payne, R. The Access Enquirer Project: From enquiry to interview. ILEA/ALFA. 1988

Percy, K. et.al. Learning in Voluntary Organisations. UDACE. 1988

R

Rogers, D. Life Chances: A working report on community education with single, homeless people. Lee Centre. 1985

Rutherford, J. & Taylor, V. The Lost Generation, Training Tomorrow, July, 1997

S

Sanderson, K. and Turner, J. Women's Training, An Evaluation of Current Provision; Women's Employment, Enterprise and Training Unit. 1992

Sargant, N. et al, The Learning Divide, NIACE/Gallup, 1997

Sargant, N. Learning and Leisure: A study of adult participation in learning and its policy implications, NIACE. 1991

Scanlan, C. L. Deterrents to Participation: An adult education dilemma. National Centre for Research in Vocational Education, Ohio State University. 1986

Schuler, T. Carnegie Third Age Enquiry, 1991

SCPR, Attitudes to Lifetime Learning, 1998

Sign of the Times, Institute of Directors report, 1998

Sinfield, S. ALFA Adult Education and Further Education Links Project: Evaluation Report. ALFA. 1987

Spurling, A. Guidance Matters, 't' magazine, June 1997

Stanton, G. & Richardson, W. Qualifications for the Future, FEDA, 1997

T

TEC National Council, A Lifetime of Learning, 1997

TEC National Council. Individual Commitment to Lifetime Learning, 1994

Thackwray, R. Black Opportunities Project. UDACE. 1988

The Learning Age, a renaissance for a New Britain, DfEE Green Paper, 1998

Toynbee, P. Equipped for Life, from Challenges Facing Future Britain, ESRC, 1998

Trim, P. Strategic Context of Training, Training Strategies (MCB UP), July 1998

Tuckett, A. Barriers to Participation in Learning, from 'For Life', CfL 1996

Tuckett, A. Towards a Learning Workforce: A policy discussion paper on adult learners at work, NIACE. 1991

U

Uden, T. The Learning Imperative, NIACE, 1998

Usher, R. & Bryant, I. Adult Education as Theory, Practice and Research: The captive triangle. Routledge. 1989

W

Webster, R. Adult education and social policy in the Republic of Ireland. Adult Education, 59, 2. 1985

West, A. Ciotti M, The New Start Strategy

West, L. Challenging the WEA: crisis, learning and purpose. Workers Education, 1. 1987

White, J. Need to Know Project: Final report. ALBSU. 1987

Wilkinson, H. et al, TimeOut: Costs & benefits of parental leave, DEMOS, 1997

Williams, J. Davis, L. & Cocking, J. Equal Opportunities and Racial Equality in Higher Education. CRE. 1989

Woodley, A. et.al. Choosing to Learn: Adults in education. SRHE/Open University Press. 1987

Woodley, A. Wagner, L. Slowey, M. and Fulton, O. Choosing to Learn: Adults in education, Open University Press. 1987

Woodrow, M. Access courses: some questions and answers. Journal of Access Studies, 1, 1986

Wylei, A. Developing Access Routes for Unwaged Women, Sandown College/REPLAN, 1987